IBM Cognos TM1 Developer's Certification Guide

Fast track your way to COG-310 certification!

James D. Miller

[PACKT] enterprise
professional expertise distilled
PUBLISHING

BIRMINGHAM - MUMBAI

IBM Cognos TM1 Developer's Certification Guide

First published: April 2011

Production Reference: 1180412

Published by Packt Publishing Ltd.
Livery Place
35 Livery Street
Birmingham B3 2PB, UK.

ISBN 978-1-84968-490-3

www.packtpub.com

Cover Image by David Gimenez (bilbaorocker@yahoo.co.uk)

Credits

Author
James D. Miller

Reviewers
Abhishek Sanghani
Sameer Sheth

Acquisition Editor
Rukshana Khambatta

Development Editor
Hyacintha D'Souza

Technical Editor
Prasad Dalvi

Project Coordinator
Alka Nayak

Proofreader
Kevin McGowan

Indexer
Rekha Nair

Graphics
Manu Joseph

Production Coordinator
Alwin Roy

Cover Work
Alwin Roy

About the Author

James D. Miller has been in the IBM Cognos TM1 consulting practice since 2004 with a primary focus on architectural design, development, and implementation of business performance management projects from inception through implementation, including the Rapid Assessment and Design (RAD) process, full-scale system design, project management, technical leadership, evaluations, and team building. Overall, he has over 30 years of relevant experience in business management, systems design and implementation, data rationalization, and proven project delivery. His key roles have been Senior Solutions Architect, Project Manager, Team and Technical Leader, and Mentor. He has also spent time as a Technical Instructor and Trainer.

James currently owns IBM certifications including IBM Certified Developer - Cognos TM1 (perfect 100 percent score on exam), IBM Certified Business Analyst - Cognos TM1, IBM Cognos TM1 Master 385 Certification (perfect 100 percent score on exam), and IBM Certified Advanced Solution Expert - Cognos TM1.

Heartfelt thanks to three very special women—Nanette, Shelby, and Paige who each in their own way contributed and supported me, and therefore, this book—Thanks!

About the Reviewer

Abhishek Sanghani majored in Computer Engineering and began his career in 2004 as a Business Intelligence and Cognos Consultant. He has worked with leading IT and Finance Services companies since then.

He pursued a Finance Management degree along with his work in the field of Cognos and BI, successfully winning awards and certifications year after year. Presently, he is working in the United Kingdom, utilizing his skills of Cognos, SQL, BI, and Data Warehousing. In his free time, he writes technical blogs and also provides training on demand.

He wrote his first book, *IBM Cognos 8 Report Studio Cookbook,* with Packt Publishing. This book covers many basic to advanced features of Report Authoring. It begins by bringing readers on the same platform and introducing the fundamental features useful across any level of reporting. Then it progresses to advanced techniques and tricks to overcome Report Studio 8 limitations.

I find this book a very useful and systematic guide to learn TM1 and prepare for the certification exam. It was a great pleasure to review this book. Thanks to James D. Miller for producing such useful work and to Packt Publishing for giving me this opportunity to review. I hope my feedback proved useful.

I would also like to thank my lovely wife Dolly for all her support.

Blog: `www.BIandCognos.blogspot.com`

Sameer Sheth has worked as a Solution-Oriented Business Intelligence Specialist with over a decade of experience in implementing Enterprise Performance Management, Business Intelligence, and Data Warehousing solutions across the Oil and Gas industry, Education Sector, Retail, Financial Spectrum, Health Care, and Airline Industry.

It is a treat to have an opportunity to formally express appreciation to Shruthi Sheth, my love, who has always been beside me during the ups and downs of life.

www.PacktPub.com

Support files, eBooks, discount offers and more

You might want to visit www.PacktPub.com for support files and downloads related to your book.

Did you know that Packt offers eBook versions of every book published, with PDF and ePub files available? You can upgrade to the eBook version at www.PacktPub.com and as a print book customer, you are entitled to a discount on the eBook copy. Get in touch with us at service@packtpub.com for more details.

At www.PacktPub.com, you can also read a collection of free technical articles, sign up for a range of free newsletters and receive exclusive discounts and offers on Packt books and eBooks.

PACKTLIB®

http://PacktLib.PacktPub.com

Do you need instant solutions to your IT questions? PacktLib is Packt's online digital book library. Here, you can access, read and search across Packt's entire library of books.

Why Subscribe?

- Fully searchable across every book published by Packt
- Copy and paste, print and bookmark content
- On demand and accessible via web browser

Free Access for Packt account holders

If you have an account with Packt at www.PacktPub.com, you can use this to access PacktLib today and view nine entirely free books. Simply use your login credentials for immediate access.

Instant Updates on New Packt Books

Get notified! Find out when new books are published by following @PacktEnterprise on Twitter, or the *Packt Enterprise* Facebook page.

Table of Contents

Preface

This book attempts to provide some general information about certification, specifics of the current IBM Cognos TM1 Developer (Test COG-310) certification exam, as well as gives a focused review of key material on the topics that you will need to master to successfully pass the current IBM Cognos TM1 Developer (Test COG-310) certification exam and earn your certification.

The chapters in this book are based upon the current certification exam topics and each will:

- Indicate the chapter topic (that it will focus on)
- Provide detail on the most important information of the chapter topic
- Show working examples (where appropriate) to reinforce concepts covered in the chapter topic
- Provide a chapter topic summary
- Give a two minute drill outlining the key points in the chapter topic
- Include a self test to help the reader determine his or her mastery of the chapter topic

Certification

Certification refers to the confirmation of certain characteristics of an object, person, or organization—Wikipedia.

As stated on `www.technicalcertifications.net`:

> *A technical certification is like a diploma, it's proof that you have the technical expertise in a particular subject area. Much like how you'd get a diploma from a college after you've demonstrated competency in the subject matter, you get a technical certification when you've passed the certification's exam.*

Professional certification formally verifies and validates that an individual has met (at least) the minimal requirements for using the tool or technology he or she becomes certified in.

Typically, obtaining a certification will require both an in-depth knowledge of a tool or technology as well as practical working experience with that tool or technology.

Benefits of certification

There can be many benefits of obtaining a professional certification. Some of them are specified in this section.

Self assessment of skills

Studying for and taking a certification exam is an experience that will provide in-depth self assessment and allow you to verify your areas of excellence and skill levels using the various features of IBM Cognos TM1.

An honest self assessment will play a key role in building your confidence to participate in or even lead complicated TM1 projects throughout your career.

Know what you know

Certification testing will allow you to clearly indentify the areas of knowledge that you are (possibly) already an expert in. Again, verifying what you already know is another great confidence builder!

Identify your areas of weakness

Certification preparation and testing will help you identify the area (or areas) where you have the least amount of expertise. These will be areas where you know it is best to acquire additional information and proficiency, before taking on that high-visibility TM1 project that might be coming up.

Resume builder

In today's job market, it has become increasingly advantageous for you to earn and maintain as many credible technical certifications as possible. Passing the Cognos TM1 certification exam lets everyone in the industry know that you are a member of a select group of professionals that have mastered the tool and technology and are ready to perform.

Acceptance and credibility in the Industry

Adding the IBM Cognos TM1 certification to your list of achievements and accomplishments proves to your current employer as well as prospective employers that you take your trade seriously and can be counted on to know how to use the tool or technology effectively, efficiently, and expertly.

Additionally, certification establishes credibility with your industry peers.

Increase overall proficiency with tool

The certification journey (preparing for and taking the exam) can increase your overall level of expertise with the tool and technology—moving you from beginner to journeyman, journeyman to expert, or expert to master.

Improvement of the tool

Your participation in the certification process is a way to take part in the promotion of standards and excellence within the industry.

Prestige

IBM holds the certification of professionals in the highest regard. According to a recent release on `www-03.ibm.com/certify/policy`:

> *IBM Professional Certification is a valuable credential. To achieve the status of an IBM Certified Professional requires an investment of both time and money. It is our goal to maintain the integrity and security of IBM certification, as well as the respect associated with IBM Professional Certification. Therefore, IBM is committed to established policies aimed at protecting your investment and the integrity of the program.*

The certification exam

As stated on `www-03.ibm.com/certify`:

> *The IBM Cognos TM1 Developer exam covers key concepts, technologies, and functionality of the Cognos products. In preparation for an exam, we recommend a combination of training and hands-on experience, and a detailed review of product documentation.*

(Note: The previous exam code for this certification was FPM-310).

Exam specifics

The IBM Cognos TM1 Developer (Test COG-310) certification exam (as of this writing) follows the same format as most IBM certification exams. The following information describes the test itself in more detail.

Length

As of this writing, the certification exam contains a total of 63 questions.

Format

As of this writing, the certification exam is multiple choice and is given electronically.

(Note: it is not currently accessible via the internet. The candidates appearing for the test must schedule an appointment to take the exam at a certified test facility).

Maximum time allowed

As of this writing, the allowed time for the certification exam allows for a total of 90 (consecutive) minutes.

Once the exam is started, time expends and does not stop until you indicate that you are done with the exam (or the total time allowed is exhausted). Once you begin the exam, if you must take a break, keep in mind that the break does not stop or pause the clock, so be prepared to complete all questions on the exam at a single sitting.

As in a written exam, you have the ability to skip or page forward and back during the time allowed.

There is no advantage for taking less time to complete the exam. Therefore, it is advised that you take the time to go back and check over the questions and answers which you finish early. This will also allow you to make sure that you answered all of the exam questions.

Questions that you do not provide an answer for are marked incorrect and will affect your total score. So, do not leave any unanswered questions! Make an educated guess if you have to!

Topics

As of this writing, the certification exam contains total nine topics. Each topic has an assigned weightage—meaning how much that particular topic is worth in the overall certification exam.

The following topics are currently covered on the exam. The weightage for each topic is provided in the brackets:

- The Components of TM1 (3 percent)
    - Identify components of the TM1 Server
- Dimensions and Cubes (16 percent)
    - Describe data points and dimensions and how they relate to cubes in TM1
    - Identify a manual process to create each type
    - Describe the use of element attributes
- TurboIntegrator (TI) (25 percent)
    - Identify uses for TurboIntegrator
    - Identify sources of input for a TI process
    - Identify variables, their types, and how they are used
    - Identify when to enable cube logging in a TI process
    - Describe when to store values versus accumulate values when loading data
    - Identify how to maintain objects created through TurboIntegrator
    - Describe how to troubleshoot TI processes
    - Aside from TI, describe various ways to load data into TM1 cubes
- Rules (25 percent)
    - Describe the advantages of using Rules versus using TurboIntegrator
    - Determine the target area of a rule
    - Identify the significance of order in rules
    - Describe the use of the DB function in rules
    - Identify ways to optimize rules
    - Identify how to trace a rule

- Advanced techniques for TI scripting (10 percent)
    - Identify the Advanced tabs in TurboIntegrator and how they are used
    - Describe the differences between the four TI scripts
    - Identify where to apply custom scripts
- Drill-through (5 percent)
    - Identify different types of data that can be drilled-to
    - Identify the steps in creating a drill-through process and rule
- Virtual and lookup cubes (10 percent)
    - Identify a lookup cube and how it might be used
    - Describe common uses of lookup cubes
- Time considerations (3 percent)
    - Identify ways to structure time dimensions
- Data presentation and reporting (3 percent)
    - Identify techniques for presenting data in a TM1 application

Minimal score required to pass

As of this writing, the certification exam has a minimum passing score of 73 percent. Since, the exam has 64 total questions, to obtain a passing score you need to answer at least 45 answers correctly.

Test languages

As of this writing, the certification exam is currently only offered in English.

Location of exam

As of this writing, the certification exam can be taken at any of the many certified testing facilities throughout the world.

A current list of certified faculties can be found online at `www.prometric.com`.

Note: Prometric is an organization that offers the most extensive, professional, and secure testing network (our channel) in the world where tests are delivered in over 160 countries in over 7,500 locations.

Sample tests

As of this writing, sample exam questions are available online at `www-03.ibm.com/certify/tests/samCOG-310.shtml`.

These questions and responses are limited in nature but do give you a very general idea of what the certification exam will be like.

Maximum attempts allowed

Although there is currently no maximum number of attempts for taking the IBM Cognos TM1 Developer (Test COG-310) certification exam, keep in mind that you will be charged in full for each attempt and no refunds are given.

Training

The IBM Cognos TM1 Developer (Test COG-310) certification exam requires both competency in TM1 as well as a thorough working knowledge of each of the major TM1 components.

This book should be used as a resource to obtain the core knowledge required to successfully pass the certification exam.

Additional research is left as an exercise for the reader.

Working experience

In addition to core knowledge, it is advised that at least some practical working experience with IBM Cognos TM1 should be acquired. Completing at least some basic development tasks in a real world environment goes a long way in preparing you for the certification testing.

What this book covers

Chapter 1, The Components of TM1, will identify and discuss each of the components of IBM Cognos TM1 that are covered in the current IBM Cognos TM1 Developer (Test COG-310) certification exam.

Chapter 2, Dimensions and Cubes, will discuss the most basic Cognos TM1 objects—Cubes and Dimensions.

Chapter 3, TurboIntegrator (TI), will explain the purpose and use of Cognos TM1 TurboIntegrator.

Chapter 4, Rules, will review the information pertaining to TM1 Rules that is important to understand when taking the current IBM Cognos TM1 Developer (Test COG-310) certification exam, including the advantages of using Rules versus TurboIntegrator as well as basic rule construction fundamentals.

Chapter 5, Advanced Techniques for TI Scripting, will discuss advanced techniques for TurboIntegrator scripting in regards to the current IBM Cognos TM1 Developer (Test COG-310) certification exam.

Chapter 6, Drill-through, will discuss the Cognos TM1 drill-through functionality in regards to the current IBM Cognos TM1 Developer (Test COG-310) certification exam. We will go over what it is, how it works, and how to construct an application with drill-through capabilities.

Chapter 7, Virtual and Lookup Cubes, will explain the definition and purpose of both virtual and lookup cubes in Cognos TM1 in regards to the current IBM Cognos TM1 Developer (Test COG-310) certification exam.

Chapter 8, Time Considerations, will discuss the importance and use of the time dimension in Cognos TM1 in regards to the current IBM Cognos TM1 Developer (Test COG-310) certification exam.

Chapter 9, Data Presentation and Reporting, will identify techniques for presenting and reporting on data in a TM1 application in regards to the current IBM Cognos TM1 Developer (Test COG-310) certification exam.

What you need for this book

Access to TM1 Server and Client software is recommended but not required. It is important to have access to the internet to be able to access TM1 documentation before taking the certification exam.

Who this book is for

This book is intended for someone who has a basic working knowledge of Cognos TM1 and is interested in obtaining a developers level certification.

Conventions

In this book, you will find a number of styles of text that distinguish between different kinds of information. Here are some examples of these styles, and an explanation of their meaning.

Code words in text are shown as follows: "Upon loading of the TM1 Add-In in Microsoft Excel, if no valid TM1 Perspectives license file (`.lic`) is found, you can only start and run TM1 Client even though you have installed TM1 Perspectives."

A block of code is set as follows:

```
['Mar 2011'] = 120;
['Mar 2011','Northeast'] = 0;
```

New terms and **important words** are shown in bold. Words that you see on the screen, in menus or dialog boxes for example, appear in the text like this: "Click on **Tools** | **Add-Ins** from the Excel menu bar."

> Warnings or important notes appear in a box like this.

> Tips and tricks appear like this.

Reader feedback

Feedback from our readers is always welcome. Let us know what you think about this book—what you liked or may have disliked. Reader feedback is important for us to develop titles that you really get the most out of.

To send us general feedback, simply send an e-mail to `feedback@packtpub.com`, and mention the book title through the subject of your message.

If there is a topic that you have expertise in and you are interested in either writing or contributing to a book, see our author guide on `www.packtpub.com/authors`.

Customer support

Now that you are the proud owner of a Packt book, we have a number of things to help you to get the most from your purchase.

Errata

Although we have taken every care to ensure the accuracy of our content, mistakes do happen. If you find a mistake in one of our books—maybe a mistake in the text or the code—we would be grateful if you would report this to us. By doing so, you can save other readers from frustration and help us improve subsequent versions of this book. If you find any errata, please report them by visiting `http://www.packtpub.com/support`, selecting your book, clicking on the **errata submission form** link, and entering the details of your errata. Once your errata are verified, your submission will be accepted and the errata will be uploaded to our website, or added to any list of existing errata, under the Errata section of that title.

Piracy

Piracy of copyright material on the Internet is an ongoing problem across all media. At Packt, we take the protection of our copyright and licenses very seriously. If you come across any illegal copies of our works, in any form, on the Internet, please provide us with the location address or website name immediately so that we can pursue a remedy.

Please contact us at `copyright@packtpub.com` with a link to the suspected pirated material.

We appreciate your help in protecting our authors, and our ability to bring you valuable content.

Questions

You can contact us at `questions@packtpub.com` if you are having a problem with any aspect of the book, and we will do our best to address it.

1
The Components of TM1

In this chapter we will identify and discuss each of the components of IBM Cognos TM1 that are covered in the current IBM Cognos TM1 Developer (Test COG-310) certification exam. The current exam assigns a weightage of 3 percent to this topic.

The components of TM1 are divided into two basic types which are:

- Client components
- Sever components

Most of these components are installed by default with a standard installation of the product, but some are not.

A standard installation is when you run the provided installation package for the version of the Cognos TM1 product you have purchased and select all of the default (already checked or selected) options.

It is also important to know that a standard install will use the following default (and recommended) values:

Admin server port number	5495
SSL port number	5498
TM1 Server port number	12345
TM1 Client message port number	Whatever the next available port number is on the installation machine
TM1 Server name	SData
Admin server host name	Installation machine name
Sample data directory for TM1 Server	`C:\Program Files\Cognos\TM1\Custom\TM1Data\PlanSamp`
Sample data directory for TM1 Perspectives/TM1 Architect	`C:\Program Files\Cognos\TM1\Custom\TM1Data\Pdata`
Security mode	TM1 Authentication

Each of the TM1 components has a particular purpose and use.

The discussion in this chapter will relate to the functionality and features of the components as it relates to the certification exam and is not meant to be a complete or exhaustive information source.

The components of TM1

First we'll get introduced to the client components of Cognos TM1.

Client components

Client components allow access to the TM1 Servers. During a default installation, the following Client components will be installed:

- TM1 Client
- TM1 Perspectives
- TM1 Architect
- TM1 API
- OLE DB Provider

What we mean by **OLE DB Provider** is simply an external software component that enables TM1 to have specialized access to OLAP data sources such as Microsoft Analysis Services and it is not directly referenced in the current IBM Cognos TM1 Developer (Test COG-310) certification exam, so we will not spend time on it.

> All of the client components can be installed on a user (client) machine as well as the (server) machine that the TM1 server components are installed. There is an advantage in having at least one client component installed on a server machine for debugging purposes, however some installation polices may inhibit this practice.

TM1 Client

The TM1 (basic) client is accessed through Microsoft Excel as an Add-In and will allow limited access to available TM1 Servers.

As a Cognos TM1 developer, you should know that a Microsoft Excel Add-In is a file that Excel can load when it starts up. The file contains program code that adds additional functionality to Excel, usually in the form of new functions.

TM1 Client does not allow administrative access to any TM1 Servers. It does not offer the ability to set up and run a local TM1 Server.

During the installation, a local version of TM1 Server is installed and can be accessed by TM1 Client, TM1 Perspectives, or TM1 Architect. A local TM1 Server gives you exclusive (administrative) access to data and objects in a set of Windows folders called **data directories**. During a TM1 Client session, only you can create, browse, and modify data or objects that a local server stores. You can also control where the data directories should be located.

Since the TM1 Client is limited in functionality, most users will choose to install and use TM1 Perspectives (TM1 Client is not covered in the exam, but you should at least be aware that it exists and what functionality it offers).

> During a default installation, TM1 Client and TM1 Perspectives are both installed. Upon loading of the TM1 Add-In in Microsoft Excel, if no valid TM1 Perspectives license file (`.lic`) is found, you can only start and run TM1 Client even though you have installed TM1 Perspectives.

TM1 Perspectives

As with TM1 Client, TM1 Perspectives is loaded and runs as an Add-In to Microsoft Excel.

With TM1 Perspectives, you can access data within TM1 Servers and you can also create and maintain TM1 objects and data on both local and remote TM1 Servers.

> It is important to be aware of the fact that with each installation of TM1 Client and TM1 Perspectives, a "personal configuration" file named `Tm1p.ini` is installed.
>
> This file is used to configure the settings for the behavior of the Add-In file within Microsoft Excel.

During a TM1 installation, you can choose to automatically load TM1 Perspectives (or TM1 Client) when Excel starts. Don't worry, if you missed this during the installation, you can perform the following easy steps:

1. Open Microsoft Excel on your desktop.
2. Click on **Tools** | **Add-Ins** from the Excel menu bar.
3. Select **Tm1p.xla.**
4. Click on **OK**.

When you click on **Add-Ins**, Microsoft Excel will most likely show you a location where it thinks the TM1P Add-In file exists.

You will almost never find the TM1P file where Excel says it should be, so you will need to browse to the location on your machine where TM1 installed the file as shown in the following screenshot:

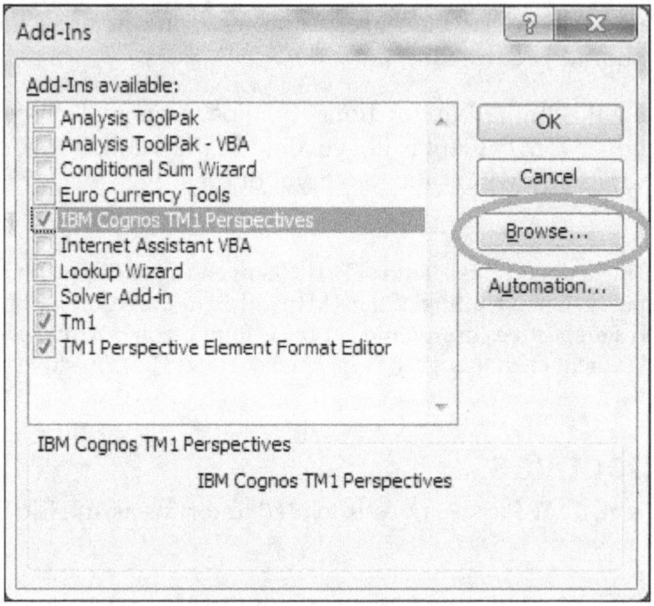

The TM1P Add-In file is usually installed during installation to the directory folder `Cognos\TM1\bin`.

Features of TM1P

The default version of `Tm1p.ini` allows multiple users to use TM1 on a given computer. `Tm1p.ini` must be present the first time a user starts TM1 on the computer, as the parameters in the system default version govern the behavior of the initial startup of the TM1 Client for each user.

After a user starts TM1 on the computer, a user-specific copy of `Tm1p.ini` is created in `%APPDATA%\Applix\TM1\Tm1p.ini`. In most cases, the full path to the `Tm1p.ini` file is:

```
C:\Documents and Settings\<user name>\Application Data\Applix\TM1\
Tm1p.ini.
```

The user-specific copy of `Tm1p.ini` accepts all parameter settings and changes for the user and governs the behavior of the TM1 Client for all subsequent user sessions of the TM1 Client.

It is important to know how to locate and configure the `Tm1p.ini` file. As you will find references to the file's purpose and settings of the file in the exam and in practice, you will have occasion to access and update it.

For your users running TM1 Clients on Windows Vista and Windows 7, application data (and therefore the `Tm1p.ini` file) is stored differently. To locate the `.ini` file, open a command line prompt, for example - **Start** | **Run** | **cmd**.

Execute the command `set APPDATA` to discover where the application data (and the `Tm1p.ini` file) is stored. The directory that is displayed will contain a directory named `Applix\TM1` that will contain `Tm1p.ini`.

> The `Tm1p.ini` file is important because that is where you can set parameters that change the user's TM1 Perspectives experience.

Some of the most interesting (and important) `.ini` file parameters are:

- `ConnectLocalAtStartup`: This parameter is set to `True` or `False` and indicates whether the client automatically attempts to connect to the local server at startup. For most users it is advantageous not to connect to the local server.
- `AdvancedRulesEditor`: This parameter is set to `True` or `False` and will indicate the type of TM1 Rules Editor that is used. The advanced Rules Editor has an enhanced interface and is somewhat more complicated and may or may not be a good choice to offer to the user, depending on that user's skill level.
- `DisplayApplications`, `DisplayChores`, `DisplayControlCubes`, `DisplayCubes`, `DisplayDimensions`, `DisplayProcesses`: These parameters (set to `True` or `False`) indicate whether TM1 Perspectives will display application folders, chores, cubes, dimensions, or processes to the user. At this point in my career I have never seen these parameters set to values other than their default values.

- `DisplayExplorerPropertiesWindow`: This is again a `True` or `False` parameter that indicates whether the **Properties** pane is visible in Server Explorer on startup. The **Properties** pane can be helpful to some users, but there is a slight performance impact with it "turned on" and visible. You may want to set this default to `False`. The **Properties** pane can be made visible later in TM1 Server Explorer by clicking on **View** and then selecting **Properties Window**.
- `DisplayReplications`: This `True/False` parameter should be set to `False` for most users. This parameter indicates whether the Replications group is visible in Server Explorer at startup.

TM1 Architect

TM1 Architect is a standalone TM1 Client application (meaning that it does not plug in to Microsoft Excel) and is used to create and maintain data and metadata on both local and remote TM1 servers.

Usually, you will see a separate menu item on your computer's desktop for accessing TM1 Architect directly as shown in the following screenshot:

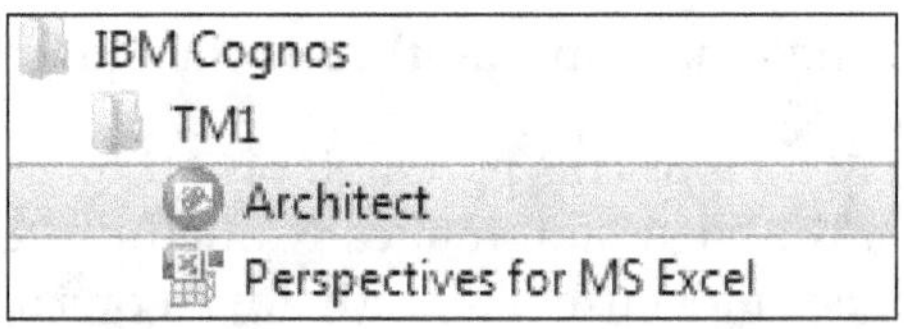

This is a tool that will be used by a TM1 user who is granted at least minimal "administrator" privileges (that is, a developer or programmer type).

It is best to use Architect when focusing on Turbo integrator scripting or possibly checking security assignments because it allows access to these features of TM1 without having to load Microsoft Excel.

> You can actually have both TM1 Perspectives and TM1 Architect open and running at the same time on your machine, accessing the same or different TM1 Servers.

Again, TM1 Architect does not hook into Microsoft Excel and cannot be used directly to create and maintain TM1 enabled Excel worksheets.

TM1 API

Along with TM1 Architect, an **application programming interface** (**API**) is installed during a default installation. This interface may be used by more experienced developers to create C++ and VB applications that interact with TM1.

> The API is not covered in the exam.

During the installation, JAVA and .NET API are also installed.

Server components

TM1 Server components are the "heart" of TM1. These components run on the machine receiving and replying to all requests from TM1 clients.

Unlike the TM1 Client components (discussed above) not all of the TM1 Server components are installed during a default or standard installation.

> A single installation of TM1 Server on a server machine can be used to run multiple TM1 Server application processes. But you will need to check your license agreement to determine if multiple servers are legal under your agreement.

The server-side TM1 components are described next.

TM1 Admin Server

The TM1 Admin Server is considered the "parent process" or "hosting process" of all other TM1 processes.

This is the process that keeps track of all other TM1 Server components running on the network. An Admin Server process runs on a computer and is known as the **Admin Host**.

> The term Admin Host is important for the certification exam.

During the installation, the TM1 Admin Server is automatically set up as a machine service for you. TM1 Servers (discussed later in this chapter) must be set up manually to be run as application services.

> TM1 Server can be installed and set up as a machine application service on a standalone machine along with the selected client components. This kind of environment is advantageous for active development.

When each TM1 Server starts, that server registers itself with the Admin Server that is running on a specified Admin Host.

TM1 Clients reference the Admin Server to determine which TM1 Servers are available on the network.

TM1 Server processes (described next) reference the `AdminHost` parameter in their own configuration file (`Tm1s.cfg`) to determine which admin host to register with. It is as follows:

```
AdminHost=mycomputername
```

If a user cannot access a TM1 application, you should verify that the TM1 Admin Host is configured correctly and is running. In some instances, you may need to stop and then restart the TM1 Admin Host (keeping in mind that all TM1 Servers currently registered with the TM1 Admin Host will need to be restarted).

Also note that, although TM1 Servers register with a single Admin Host, all TM1 clients (TM1 Client, TM1 Perspectives, and TM1 Architect) can reference multiple Admin Hosts simply by listing them all under **Login Parameters/ Admin Host** in the upper left of the **TM1 Options** dialog.

In the following screenshot, three admin hosts (host1, host2 and host3) are listed and therefore, all TM1 Servers currently running on these machines will be visible in these users' TM1 Server Explorer:

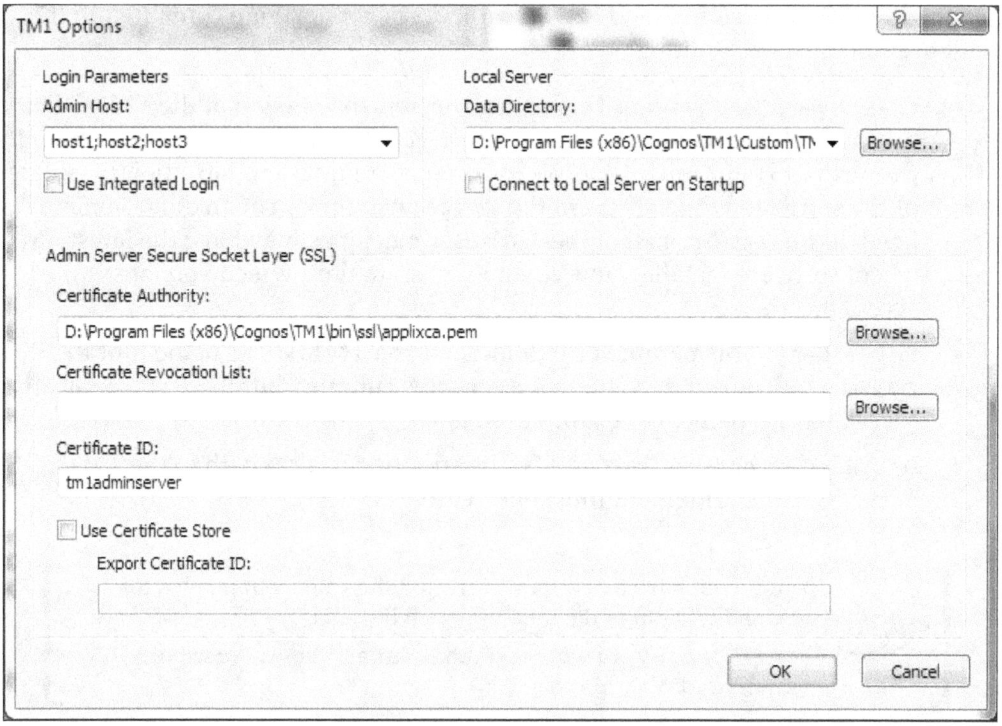

TM1 Server configuration files by default reside in the TM1 Server's `SData` folder.

The `SData` folder can be reviewed for file and timestamp information as required to note the last time these objects were updated.

> The `SData` folder is the location on the server where all of the server's object files (cubes, dimensions, processes, and so on.) also reside. This is also the location where TM1 log and error files are written to unless a "logs folder" is set up in the TM1 Server's CFG or configuration file.

TM1 CFG

The TM1 configuration (`.cgf`) file is a simple text file that can be accessed and updated using a simple text editor like Windows notepad.

> While changing parameters in the configuration file, you will need to stop and restart the TM1 Server to see the effects of the changes.

Some of the most interesting (and important) parameters that are contained in the configuration file are as follows:

- `ClientVersionMaximum`: This parameter sets the version of the TM1 Client components that can access this TM1 Server. This is important because, in the production environment, a TM1 Server may be upgraded to a newer version of the software while others in the server farm remain at an older version level. In this case, not all of the TM1 user machines may have the latest TM1 Client software installed and you may wish to limit which versions can access this server.
- `ServerName`: This parameter will indicate the TM1 Server name (not the physical machine name where the server is running, but the TM1 application server service name. For example "finance_1").
- `DataBaseDirectory`: This will be the specific physical path to the TM1 Server's `SData` folder and must end with a \.

> You do not have to use quotes around the value, but it helps for readability. Both of the following will be valid:
> `="c:\company_finance_data\sdata\"` or `=c:\company_finance_data\sdata\`

- `LoggingDirectory`: This will be the specific physical path to the TM1 Server's `logging` folder and must end with a \. If no `logging` folder is provided, TM1 Server will write its logs, errors, and exceptions to the specified `SData` folder (described above).

> It is a good practice to specify a logging directory.

- `AdminHost`: This is the physical machine name on which the TM1 Server is installed and running.

TM1 Server

The TM1 Server is a process that manages all requests from all TM1 clients. It loads the names of all available permanent objects (cubes, dimensions, and so on) into the machine's memory and responds to client requests by performing calculations, consolidations, and updates as required. Refer to the following screenshot:

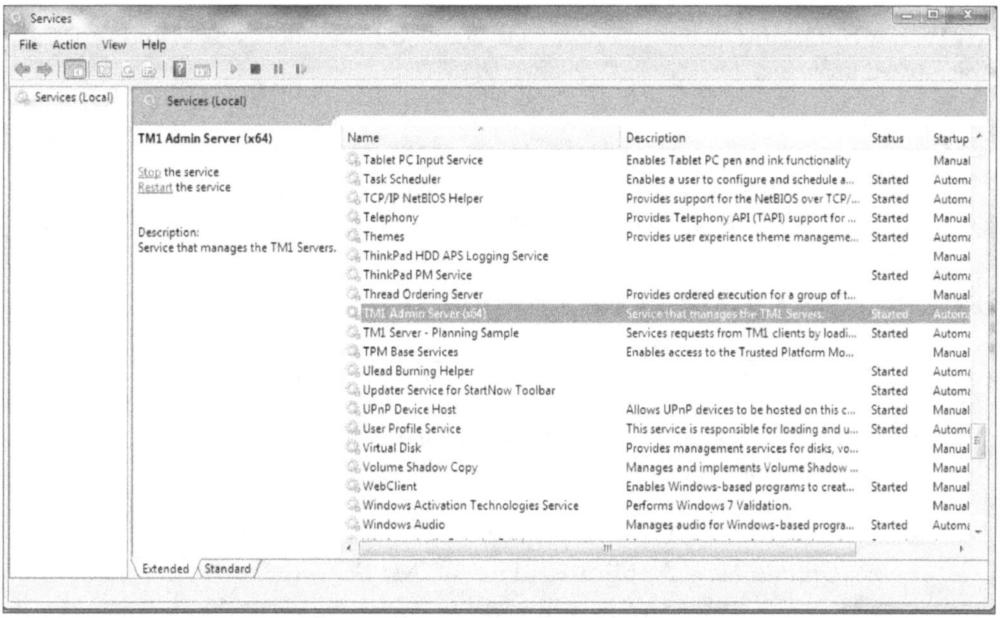

The TM1 Server also manages security-granting or denying access to server objects and maintaining a log of changes to the database.

> There may be any number of TM1 Server processes running on the network. The number of TM1 Server processes is only limited by the memory available to them. As mentioned earlier, each TM1 Server must be manually set up to run as a machine application service.

Multiple TM1 Servers can be viewed and accessed through a single TM1 Server Explorer (via TM1 Client, TM1 Perspectives, TM1 Architect, or TM1 Web) if it is configured properly.

TM1 Web

TM1 Web refers to all the web server components required to access the TM1 Servers (and their data) using a web browser.

TM1 Web is not a part of the standard installation and you must perform a TM1 Web installation to install these components.

TM1 Web is commonly used to access TM1-enabled Excel worksheets and reports using a web browser.

> In order for worksheets and reports to be available to the users via their web browsers, the worksheets and reports must have a "reference" to them set up in an application folder.

Setting up a worksheet reference

To set up a reference for a TM1 worksheet or report, the developer must publish each of them to the application folder. This is accomplished as follows:

1. Open the worksheet or report to be published in Microsoft Excel.
2. Click on the TM1 menu.
3. Select **Save Workbook On TM1 Server...**.
4. Select **Upload New Application File to TM1 Server...**.
5. Navigate to (and select) the application folder location on the server where you want the file to reside.

> After publishing the worksheet, make sure that the file security is appropriately set (the default is private).

Two reports published to a TM1 Server are shown in the following screenshot. The secured or "private" report is visible only to the TM1 user who published the report and is designated with a "key icon":

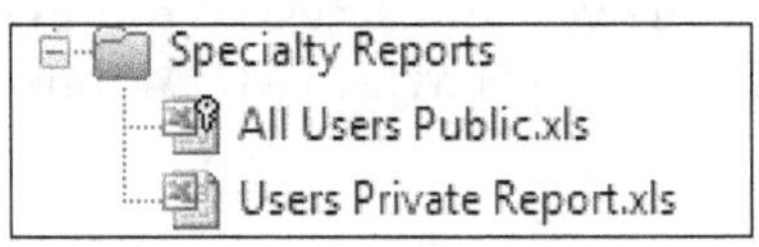

TM1 Top

TM1 Top is a TM1 "utility" that enables you to dynamically monitor and manage threads (active user sessions) running in an instance of a Windows or UNIX TM1 Server.

The current version of TM1 Top runs only on a Windows system and is available only with the Windows installation of TM1.

> To monitor a UNIX TM1 Server, use the TM1 Installation Wizard to install TM1 Top on a Windows system and then configure TM1 Top to connect to the UNIX TM1 Server. When the `AdminHost` and `ServerName` parameters are pointing to a UNIX machine, TM1 Top will monitor the UNIX environment. See the IBM Cognos TM1 Operations Guide for details on configuring the `Tm1Top.ini` file—IBM.

When TM1 Top is installed, it sets up a `Tm1Top.ini` file that you can configure to point to the TM1 Server that you want to monitor. Using a text editor such as Microsoft's notepad, you can edit the file and provide your server name and the machine (or admin host) that the server is running on. In addition, if you provide a log file name, TM1 will write a snapshot of its display to the file in regular intervals (specified by the **logperiod** parameter):

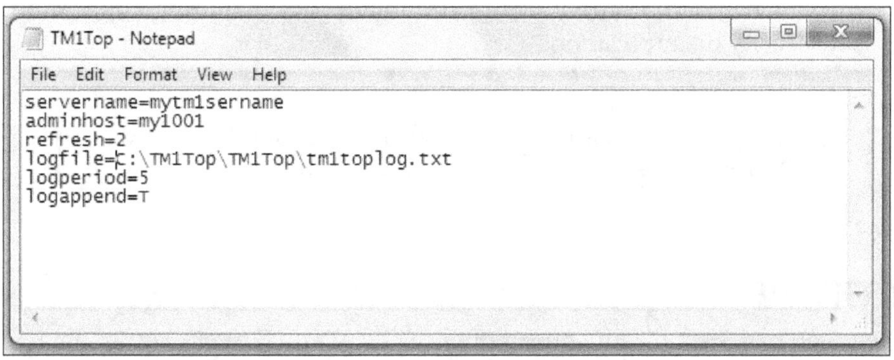


```
servername=mytm1sername
adminhost=my1001
refresh=2
logfile=C:\TM1Top\TM1Top\tm1toplog.txt
logperiod=5
logappend=T
```

> If you are a TM1 user with administrative access, TM1 Top may be used to cancel any current TM1 user thread. This practice should be approached with caution as a thorough understanding of what the user thread is doing and the reason for canceling it is recommended.

The following screenshot shows a running TM1 Top session. Note that the two active user sessions shown in the screenshot are actually TM1 Admin Server sessions—not individual TM1 users.

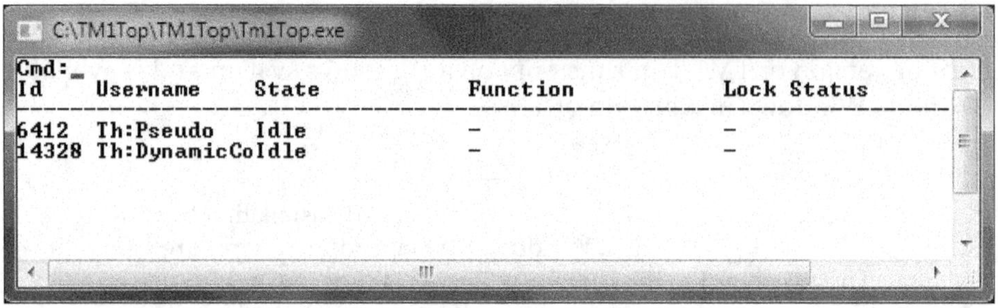

TM1 Contributor

This component is installed by default only as a part of the TM1 Contributor installation, not as a part of the standard TM1 installation.

TM1 Contributor includes:

- **TM1 Contributor Web Client**: This is a web-based client used to browse and contribute data within the TM1 Contributor workflow application.
- **TM1 Contributor Administration**: This is a configuration, design, and management tool used by administrators to build planning applications and set security on applications.

> TM1 Contributor is not a part of the IBM Cognos TM1 Developer (Test COG-310) certification exam.

Summary

We have seen that TM1 provides a set of both Client and Server components. Most of them are installed by default during a standard TM1 installation. Each has their own features and purpose. Most of the components' appearance and behaviours can be customized for each individual TM1 user.

The Client components can be used to access multiple TM1 Servers on the network.

TM1 Top is a utility that can be configured and used to monitor a TM1 Server.

A basic understanding of each component (Client as well as Server) including the knowledge of how they are installed and customised, is required to do well with the IBM Cognos TM1 Developer (Test COG-310) certification exam. This chapter provides that information.

In the next chapter we will examine the most basic Cognos TM1 objects; cubes and dimensions.

Two minute drill

In this chapter, we got to know about the following points:

- The components of TM1 are divided into two basic types which are "Client components" and "Sever components".
- Most of the TM1 components are installed by default when you perform a standard installation of the product, but some are not.
- Each component has a particular purpose and use.
- Client components allow access to the TM1 Servers.
- Client components include TM1 Client, TM1 Perspectives, and TM1 Architect.
- TM1 Client is accessed through Microsoft Excel as an Add-In.
- TM1 Client will only allow limited access to available TM1 Servers.
- TM1 Client and TM1 Perspectives are loaded and run as an Add-In to Microsoft Excel.
- With TM1 Perspectives, you can create and maintain TM1 objects and data on both local and remote TM1 Servers.
- `Tm1p.ini` is a file that allows changing the behaviors of TM1 Client and TM1 Perspectives.
- TM1 Architect is a standalone TM1 Client application.
- TM1 Architect will be used by a TM1 user who is granted at least minimal "administrator" privileges (that is, a developer or programmer type).
- TM1 Admin Server is considered the "hosting process" of all other TM1 processes.
- TM1 Admin Server is automatically set up as a machine service for you.
- TM1 Servers must be manually set up to run as application services.
- Each TM1 Server has an `SData` folder and can be reviewed for file and timestamp information.

- TM1 Server is a process that manages all requests from all TM1 Clients.
- TM1 Server also manages security.
- TM1 Web refers to the entire web server components required to access the TM1 Servers (and their data) using a web browser.
- TM1 Web is commonly used to access TM1-enabled Excel worksheets and reports using a web browser.
- Worksheets and reports must have a "reference" to them set up in an application folder.
- TM1 Top is a "utility" that enables you to monitor and manage the threads created by both TM1 Server and TM1 users.
- TM1 Contributor is not a part of the IBM Cognos TM1 Developer (Test COG-310) certification exam.

Self test

- **Question**: What are the two types of TM1 components?

  Response: Client components and Server components.

- **Question**: Name the main Client components that are installed during a default TM1 installation process.

  Response: TM1 Client, TM1 Perspectives,TM1 Architect,TM1 API, and OLEDB Provider.

- **Question**: Describe the purpose of the `Tm1p.ini` file?

  Response: It is used to change the behaviors of TM1 Client and TM1 Perspectives.

- **Question**: What are the differences between TM1 Client and TM1 Perspectives?

  Response: TM1 Client and TM1 Perspectives both are run as an Add-In to Microsoft Excel but TM1 Client is very basic and is mainly used for just accessing data in TM1. TM1 Perspectives can be used to update and change TM1 objects.

- **Question**: What is the purpose of the TM1 Admin Server?

  Response: To manage all running TM1 Server processes.

- **Question**: What is an Admin Host?

  Response: It is the parent TM1 process—TM1 Admin Server—and manages all requests from all TM1 Server processes.

- **Question**: What is the number of TM1 Servers that can be viewed and accessed through a single TM1 Server Explorer?

  Response: Multiple TM1 Servers can be viewed and accessed through a single TM1Server Explorer (via TM1 client, TM1 Perspectives, TM1 Architect, or TM1 Web) if it is configured properly.

- **Question**: What does it mean when we say "TM1 Web"?

  Response: TM1 Web refers to the entire web server components required to access the TM1 servers (and their data) using a web browser.

- **Question**: What is the method to make a worksheet or report available via a user's web browser and TM1 Web?

  Response: A reference for a TM1 worksheet or report must be established by "publishing" it to an application folder using TM1 Perspectives.

- **Question**: What is the TM1 Server port used when a standard installation is done?

  Response: 12345.

- **Question**: What is the Admin Host?

  Response: The physical name of the machine that the TM1 Server is installed and running on.

- **Question**: When you make a change to the TM1 configuration (`.cfg`) file, do you see the changes reflected as soon as you save the file?

  Response: No, the changes must be made, the file must be saved, and the TM1 Server must be stopped and restarted to see the changes reflected.

- **Question**: What is the `VersionMaximum` parameter used for?

  Response: This parameter, found in the TM1 configuration (`.cfg`) file, is used to limit the number of TM1 Client versions that can access the TM1 Server.

- **Question**: If no logging folder is provided what happens to the TM1 Server logs and errors?

  Response: If no logging folder is set in the TM1 configuration (`.cgf`) file, TM1 Server will write its logs, errors, and exceptions to the specified `SData` folder.

2

Dimensions and Cubes

In this chapter, we will discuss the most basic Cognos TM1 objects:

- Cubes
- Dimensions

We will identify and explain each of these objects—focusing on the information covered in the current IBM Cognos TM1 Developer (Test COG-310) certification exam.

The current certification exam assigns a weightage of 16 percent to this topic.

Introduction to cubes and dimensions

What tables are to relational databases in the way cubes are to TM1. Almost all data stored in TM1 is stored in and accessed from cubes.

There are two ways to create cubes:

- **Empty cube**: You can create an empty cube by selecting (at least) two dimensions from the list of existing dimensions in the **Creating Cube** window to create a new cube with no data.
- **External data sources**: You can create a cube and load it with data by using TurboIntegrator to identify and map dimensions and data from an external data source to a new or existing cube (of course, this requires some expertise using TurboIntegrator).

Each and every TM1 cube must have at least two dimensions and a maximum of 256 dimensions.

Without dimensions, there will be no cubes. So let's start the discussion with dimensions!

Dimensions

You create a cube with dimensions, and dimensions identify how to organize the information or data that you want to track and report on. Each element in each dimension identifies the location (or "x-y coordinate") of a cell in a cube.

Data is loaded into cube cells. A cell is identified by the intersection of dimensions.

Common dimensions are time periods, products, markets, customers, suppliers, promotion conditions, raw materials, manufacturing plants, transportation methods, media types, and so on.

When you create a dimension, you identify the leaf-level elements that make up the dimension and, optionally, any hierarchies (consolidations) of the elements within the dimension.

Dimension names can have a maximum of 256 characters.

> You should always use descriptive dimension names. Your dimension names should be "user friendly" to the average business user (not the average TM1 developer!). You should avoid using special characters and always include "white space" between terms. For example, I like "Headquarters PL Account" rather than "HQ_PL_Acct".

There are four ways to create dimensions:

- **Use the Dimension Editor**: This is the most basic method of creating a dimension. You simply add your elements (as well as creating and rearranging consolidations of your elements) manually within the Dimension Editor window. You should know that elements may be "copied and pasted" into the Dimension Editor from outside data stores (such as a Microsoft Excel worksheet).
- **TurboIntegrator**: This is by far the most common method of creating dimensions. You can use your custom **TurboIntegrator** processes to import element names from an ASCII, ODBC, cube view, or dimension subset source. You can also (with some program scripting) create multiple dimensions and establish consolidations within those dimensions. Most often the TurboIntegrator scripts are written in such a way that they can be reused to perform regular maintenance on the dimensions that they originally created.
- **Importing data into a new cube**: Of course, it should also be mentioned that TurboIntegrator processes can be used to map input rows from a data source to a cube and then identify the input columns that supply the cell values and the elements that identify the cell location.

- **Dimension worksheets**: Finally, an older, less flexible method of creating dimensions is the use of modified Microsoft Excel worksheets (designated as dimension worksheets) to list the elements and hierarchical relationships for one dimension. This method seems to be seldom used anymore and is not covered in the exam.

Elements

Dimensions are made up of elements. TM1 currently supports three types of elements:

Element	Description
Numeric	Numeric elements identify the lowest-level detail in a dimension. In a cube that contains only numbers, TM1 defines all the lowest-level elements as numeric.
Consolidated	Consolidations are aggregations or rollups of lower-level detail elements.
String	String elements store text strings in the cells. To include a string in a cell in a cube, the element from the last dimension defining the cell must be a string element. TM1 treats string elements that occur in any dimension other than the last one as numeric elements.

Key points are numeric elements which can be referred to as simple element types and identify the lowest level in a dimension hierarchy and consolidation elements. They are created strictly to calculate an aggregation.

Editing element properties

If you have added elements of a specified type to your dimension and you wish to change it, you can edit the element properties to assign a new weight to the element of a consolidation, or to change the element type (of a simple element).

Keep in mind that you cannot change the element type of any consolidated elements and you cannot assign an element weight to any instance of an element that is not a member of a consolidation.

Warning! Once your dimension is a part of the cube that contains data you must be very careful while changing any element properties to prevent loss of any data loaded to that element.

The **Dimension Element Properties** dialog is used to make the changes to the selected element.

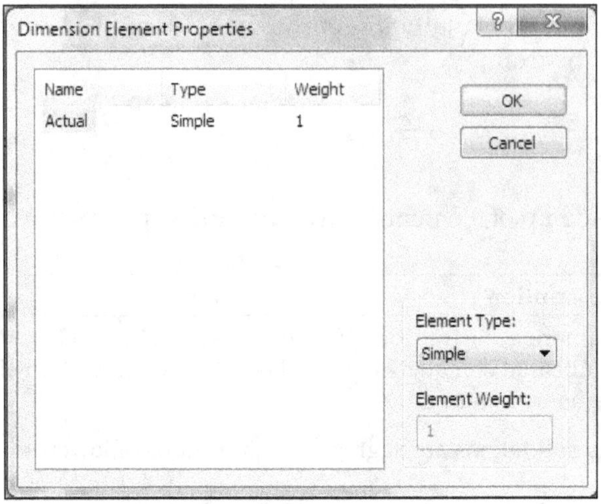

Aggregations

One of the key things to understand is that TM1 will quickly and efficiently aggregate numeric element values for your reporting.

For example, consider a simple calculation such as aggregating (or rollup) the values of a group of accounts into one amount. This is accomplished through **aggregation**. Aggregation is automatically applied in TM1 while building a dimension using something called hierarchies.

A **hierarchy** is a way to organize data at different levels of aggregation.

It is important to understand that aggregation calculations will be based upon each element's "weight". IBM refers to this as the element's **weight factor**. Weight factors determine the contribution of an element to a consolidation.

The default element weight is one.

Just about any weight factor can be assigned to an element and it is not uncommon for an element to have a negative weight factor, causing it to be subtracted from the total aggregation amount. Therefore, to show a negative value, a developer can assign a negative weight to an element.

Consolidating using dimension hierarchies

The data you import into a cube provides a snapshot of your business at a specific level of detail. For example, you might import your weekly or monthly sales for your surfboards in dollars for a specific city in which they were sold. The dimension elements that identify these data points are simple or leaf-level elements in each dimension. These data points can be surfboards sold in one week and in a particular city.

By using dimension hierarchies, you can easily aggregate numeric data into categories that are meaningful in your analyses. Each category corresponds to an aggregation of detail for two or more elements in a dimension. For example, you could create quarterly elements that sum monthly sales amounts. In TM1, elements that represent aggregations are called **consolidated elements** or **consolidations**.

We'll speak more about hierarchies later in this chapter.

Element attributes

In addition, to define an element's type (numeric, consolidation, or string), elements can have attributes defined for them. If elements identify data in a cube, then think of the element attributes describing the elements themselves.

For example, let us say that some of your users would like to display an account using the account name followed by the account number. Other users would like to display only the account name. You can define an alias attribute for each of these requirements. In fact, you can define as many alias attributes as you need.

I can have an account number of "01-0000-00001" and define multiple aliases so that the user can view the element as any of the following:

- "01-0000-00001"
- "01-0000-00001 – Long Surfboard"
- "Long Surfboard"

Some interesting uses for attributes include:

- To define features of elements. For example, an employee may have attributes that include "title", "hire date", or "department"
- To provide alternative or "friendly" names, or aliases. For example, an accounting code of "02-0000-00001" may have an alias of "salary and wages"
- To control the display format for the numeric data. This is a clever idea and we will drill into this later in this chapter

An alias attribute may also be used to present data in different languages!

You can select elements by attribute value in the Subset Editor. You can also display element names in TM1 windows using their aliases.

To create attributes and assign attribute values, you use the Attributes Editor.

When adding attributes using the Attributes Editor, you will notice that it "defaults" to an attribute type of string, so be careful to select the desired type before proceeding. In most cases, TurboIntegrator processes will be the tool used to add, update, and delete your dimension attributes. You use the following programming functions:

- `AttrInsert`: To add a new attribute
- `AttrPutN` or `AttrPutS`: To update the attribute which can be numeric or string value
- `AttributeDelete`: To remove an existing attribute

A key point to know is that, if you try to view or update dimensions attributes and there are a large number of elements in the dimension when you open the Attributes Editor, you will receive a message as shown in the following screenshot:

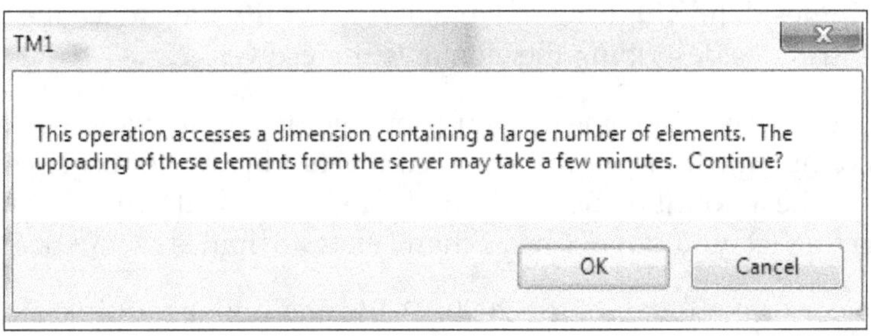

> Do not continue! You can potentially lock your TM1 session for a long time.

The alternative is to access the attributes of this dimension through the attributes cube instead, as it is much faster:

1. Select **View | Display Control Objects**.
2. Open the cube called `}ElementAttributes_dimension`.
3. Modify the required fields like in any cube!

This is another important point. The `}ElementAttributes` cubes are known as Cognos TM1 **control cubes**. These cubes are automatically generated by TM1. As an application developer you can either create a new (lookup) cube or use a control cube to look up data, depending upon your needs. Lookup and control cubes are discussed later in this chapter.

Some key attribute terminology and concepts you should be able to recognize are descriptive attributes, alias attributes, and when to use an attribute versus an additional element. Let us briefly touch on these.

Descriptive attributes

Descriptive attributes are simply the attributes which are data that describe the data.

For example, consider some attributes for selecting a surfboard:

Elements	Length	Finish	Fin
Surfboard 1	6.0	None	Single
Surfboard 2	6.6	Base yellow	Triple
Surfboard 3	7.0	Green	Dual
Surfboard 4	7.6	None	Dual
Surfboard 5	8.0	Blue wave	Single

Alias attributes

These attributes provide alternative names for elements:

Elements	Description	Full Name
01-0000-00001	Employee wages	01-0000-00001 - Employee Wages
01-0000-00002	Stock bonus	01-0000-00002 - Stock Bonus
01-0000-00003	Travel expense	01-0000-00003 - Travel Expense

It can be tempting to add many attributes to describe your elements and in most cases this is fine as you can filter your data by attribute value, however you should consider how your data is going to be used and presented. Sometimes it is more appropriate to create elements rather than attributes and sometimes even additional dimensions.

For example, board length is an attribute of surfboard models. The 6.6 boards often outsell the other length boards. If you create one element per board and another dimension with elements for each length, you can use TM1 to track surfboard sales by the length of the board. If you combine sales into a single board length, you might lose valuable detail.

Display format attributes

As I mentioned earlier in this chapter, a clever use for element attributes is formatting what is displayed in the Cube Viewer. When you create a dimension, an attribute named **format** is created for you automatically by TM1. This attribute can be used to set a display format for each individual numeric element.

> It is recommended that you select display formats for only one dimension in a cube, for the measures you track. Remember, you can still select a format in the Cube Viewer window that applies to cells whose elements do not have a display format defined.

Display format attributes can also be set programmatically with a TurboIntegrator process using the `AttrPutS` function. Just remember to add the `c:` to the format string to indicate that it is a custom format:

```
AttrPutS('c:###,###.00', myDimensioName, myElementName, 'Format');
```

Referring to the IBM Cognos documentation, you see that the numeric data can be displayed in the following formats:

Currency	Numbers will appear with a currency symbol and the number of decimal places (precision).	$10.00
General	Numbers will appear with a specified number of decimal places.	-10
Percentage	Numbers will appear as percentages, with a specified number of decimal place.	10.00%
Scientific	Numbers will appear in exponential form, with a specified number of decimal places.	1.0e+001
Date	Numbers will appear as a date string. There are a number of date formats available.	Jun 31, 2002
Time	Numbers will appear as a time string. There are a number of time formats available.	8:53:30 A
Comma	Allows the placement of commas.	7,000,000
Custom	Custom defined format.	Can be Custom

The Cube Viewer will display the format to use:

1. Elements in the column dimension are checked for formatting.
2. Elements are checked in the row dimension for display formats.
3. Elements are checked in the title dimension for display formats (left to right).

The current view formatting is used

Creating dimensions using the Dimension Editor window

The most common, although time consuming method of creating dimensions, is using the Dimension Editor window. This is an approach that might be used for smaller, slow moving dimensions. In real-world enterprise applications, larger dimensions (such as P&L accounts) may be created and maintained by the TurboIntegrator processes using source files from a client's GL system.

Another time when you may use the Dimension Editor to create a dimension is during a "proof of concept" or "prototyping" effort when you want to generate something quickly to show and then to throw it away.

Follow the next steps to create dimensions using the Dimension Editor window:

1. Click on **Dimensions** | **Create New Dimension** and the **Dimension Editor** will open.
2. Click on **Edit** | **Insert Element** and the **Dimension Element Insert** dialog box will open.
3. To add a consolidated element, do the following:
   a. Type **My Total** in the **Insert Element Name** field.
   b. Select **Consolidated** from the **Element Type** list.
   c. Click on **Add**.
   d. Click on **OK**.

4. **My Total** now appears as the first element of the dimension, which is a consolidated element. Now you can add child elements to the **My Total** element by following the next steps:
   a. Select the **My Total** element.
   b. Click on **Edit** | **Insert Child and** the **Dimension Element Insert** dialog box will open.
   c. In the **Insert Element Name** field, type **value1** and click on **Add**.
   d. In the **Insert Element Name** field, type **value2** and click on **Add**.
   e. The dialog box now contains two children of **My Total**, each with a default weight of one.
   f. Click on **OK**.
5. The **Dimension Editor** shows the new elements as children of **My Total**.
6. Click on **Dimension** | **Save** | **Dimension Save.**
7. As dialog box opens, enter a dimension name and click on **Save**.

The new dimension gets displayed in the list of dimensions on the server.

After creating your dimension with the Dimension Editor, you can then use it to make modifications to that dimension. You can:

- Add siblings to existing elements.
- Add children to existing elements.
- Rearrange the hierarchy structure (such as repositioning elements within consolidations).
- Delete elements from the dimension.
- Delete elements from consolidations.
- Edit element properties, such as changing the weight of an element within a consolidation.

- Rearrange the order of elements in the dimension.

> A couple of things you need to know about the Dimension Editor:
> - Element types are listed as simple, consolidated, and string.
> - Remember that simple is a term used for numeric.

The element weight shows a default as 0.0 but if you leave this, it will add the element with a default weight of 1.0.

You can copy elements from almost any source (other dimension, text file, Microsoft Excel worksheet) and paste them into the Dimension Editor to add multiple elements in one step.

You can use "drag and drop" to move elements around within the dimension.

"Delete Element" removes the element from the dimension while "Delete Element from Consolidation" removes the element from its "parent element" and not from the dimension unless that element is only defined as a child of that parent.

Ordering elements in a dimension

The order of elements in a dimension is very important! When you add elements to a dimension, TM1 assigns an index number to each element automatically. TM1 uses the index internally to keep track of the elements. Keep in mind that as elements are deleted, those indexes will be reassigned to other elements! If you (or TM1) change the order of elements in a dimension, any processes or applications that reference the element index values will return new and possibly unexpected values.

However, you can reset the order of the elements in your dimension to re-determine the index value for each element in a dimension. One way to perform this is through the Dimension Editor. You simply order the elements as you want them to appear in the dimension (see the sort options functionality of the **Dimension Editor).**

Next, click on **Set Dimension Order** | **Dimension** | **Save**. When the sorting property of the dimension is set to **Automatic**, TM1 prompts you to change the sorting property to **Manual**. When the sorting property of the dimension is set to **Manual**, TM1 inserts any elements you added to the dimension wherever you manually positioned them in the Dimension Editor.

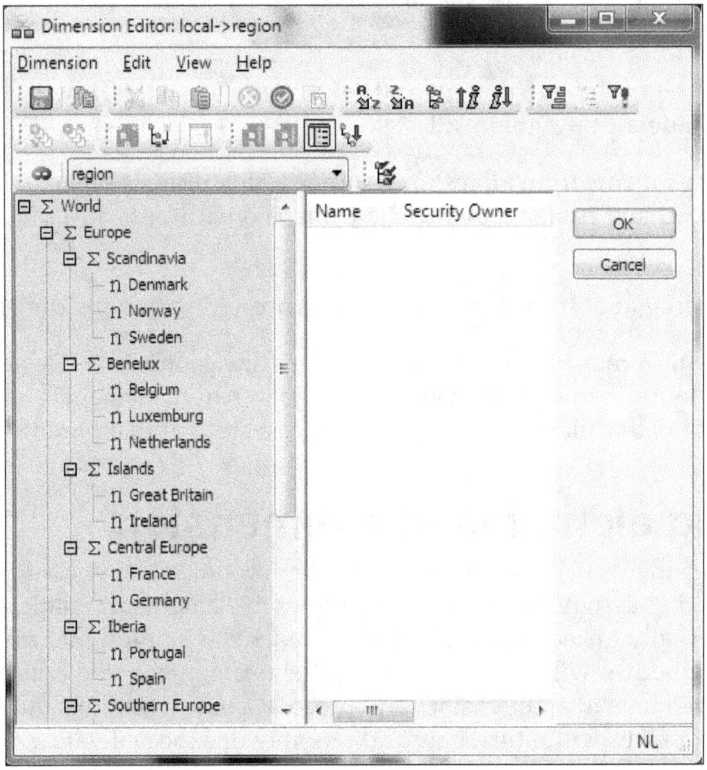

Finally, click on **Yes** to save the new dimension order and set the dimension sorting property to **Manual**.

You can set the order of elements even when the **Dimension Editor** displays only a subset of all dimension elements. For example, if you have a large dimension, you might want to alter and set the order of just a few elements. Be aware that when you set the order of elements with just a subset of elements displayed in the **Dimension Editor**, the entire dimension is affected.

Setting the order of dimension elements from the Server Explorer

You can also set the order of dimension elements directly from TM1 Server Explorer (right-click on the dimension in the Server Explorer and then select **Set Elements Order**). You select a sorting property for the dimension from these three automatic sort orders:

- **Name**: Sorts elements alphabetically
- **Level**: Sorts elements by hierarchy level
- **Hierarchy**: Sorts elements according to the dimension hierarchy

After you set the sorting property, TM1 inserts the elements you added to the dimension according to their position within the sort order.

Cubes

The mechanics of manually creating a cube is simple; from the TM1 Server Explorer you can just click on **Cubes | Create New Cube** and then fill in or select the required information.

Designing a cube structure is a different exercise and it is not a direct part of the material covered in the current IBM Cognos TM1 Developer (Test COG-310) certification exam, so here are just some very basic guidelines to use in your cube structure design:

- What are the measures you want to track?
- What is the base time interval: days, weeks, months?
- Is there a geographic dimension?
- Will your measures vary by customer and product?
- Is there a scenario or version dimension?
- How do the dimension elements need to be consolidated?
- What data needs to be associated with the element data in the form of attributes?
- Are there any specific display formats for the measures in your cubes?

Some interesting and therefore important facts about the mechanics of cube creation that you need to be aware of for the exam are:

- If you do not provide a name for your cube, TM1 names the new cube as **Unnamed**.
- You can always create cubes on your local server but you must be a TM1 administrator to create cubes on remote servers.
- You should always include your measures dimension as the last dimension in your cube.
- You should (try to) order your dimensions from the smallest and sparsest of dimensions to the largest and most dense dimensions.
- The order of your dimensions can impact the performance of your cube.
- You must select at least two dimensions. The maximum number of dimensions is 256.
- Setting up the measures and a time dimension as cube properties is not required for TM1. This feature is offered if an external OLAP client is going to access your TM1 cube as a data source.
- By default, TM1 loads all cubes into memory when a server starts.
- If you have certain cubes that are infrequently accessed (such as historical data cubes), you can set those cubes to load only when a client attempts to access the cube data. This is done using cube properties through TM1 server explorer.
- TM1 includes a feature that lets an admin user change the order of dimensions in a cube, consuming less memory and improving performance.

When you change the order of dimensions in a cube with this feature, TM1 does not change the actual order of dimensions in the cube structure. TM1 does change the way in which dimensions are ordered internally on the server, but any rules, functions, or applications referencing the cube remain valid because the cube structure is not changed. You should be sure to optimize the order of dimensions in a cube only in a development environment while you are trying to determine optimal cube configuration because significant memory resources are required for the TM1 Server to reconfigure the order of dimensions in a cube and a Read lock is put on the server, locking all user requests while the re-order is performed.

Loading cubes

Once your cube is created, you will want to load it with data. Data can be loaded using Excel worksheets or manually through the cube viewer. If you choose to enter your data manually, TM1 provides a feature called **spreading**. Using spreading, an application developer can quickly populate a large number of cells in a cube with the same data.

The most flexible and effective method to load a cube with data is through the use of a custom TurboIntegrator process. This process can read data from any number of data sources such as such another TM1 cube, an external database, or a flat ASCII file. The use of TurboIntegrator processes is discussed in next chapter of this book.

Before data can be loaded, the data's destination within the cube should be first cleared or "zeroed out".

Depending upon the detail level of the data to be loaded and the structure of the cube that the data is to be loaded into, you may need to accumulate or consolidate the data up to the level supported by the cube to load it.

Viewing cube characteristics

Within the Cognos TM1 Server Explorer, you can select **View** and then **Properties Window**. This will display the **Properties Window** (on the right side) in explorer.

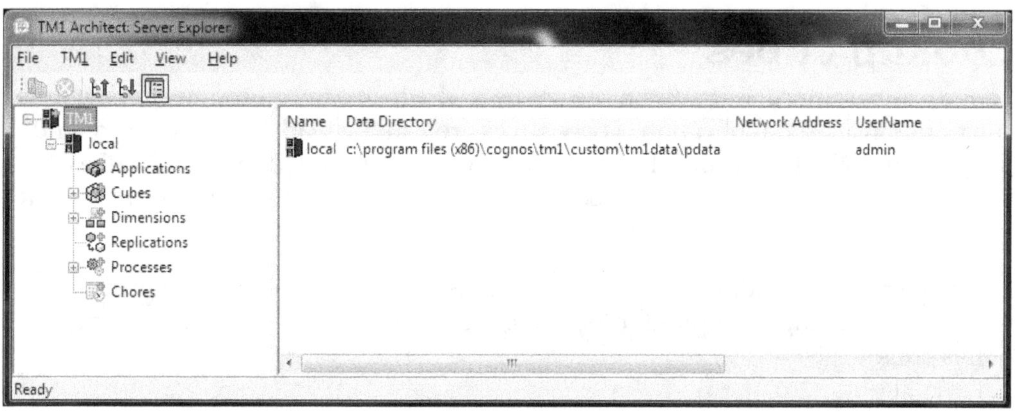

Now, when you click on **Cubes** in **Server Explorer**, TM1 will display a list of all the cubes in the instance along with each cube's:

- Owner
- Replication server
- Memory it (currently) uses when loaded
- If the cube is private or public
- The number of dimensions in this cube
- The name of its measures dimension (if one has been assigned)
- The name of its time dimension (if one has been assigned)

You can also click on an individual cube and view similar information about the specific cube. This information includes:

- List of all dimensions that make up that cube
- The order of the dimensions that make up that cube
- Memory each dimension (currently) uses
- If the dimensions are private or public
- The current number of subsets defined on each dimension
- The current number of elements in each dimension

Lookup cubes

Lookup cubes are cubes that you can set up and which can be used to support other cubes within a TM1 application. These cubes are usually read-only to the user and may contain calculations or reference data that are then pulled into other cubes using TM1 rules. Lookup cubes can also be used to load data into the application without locking the cubes that the users see and use.

Exchange rates is one of the uses of lookup cubes in TM1. Using the DB formula, many other existing examples for lookup cubes are examined in another chapter of this book.

Control cubes

The cubes that TM1 itself uses to perform certain activities are called **control cubes**. These activities are:

- Security
- Client and group administration

- Object attribute and properties control
- Performance monitoring
- Hold tracking by username

All control cubes are named with a first character of } and are by default not visible within in TM1 Server Explorer. These cubes can be made visible by selecting **View** and then **Display Control Objects**.

Security

The security control cubes are used to apply security privileges for TM1 objects including cubes, dimensions, processes, and chores to user groups on a TM1 Server. Usually, these control cubes are populated with the privileges assigned in the TM1 Security Assignments window, but you can also apply privileges directly in the control cubes (remember that, you cannot apply privileges to the ADMIN group; this group always has ADMIN privileges to all objects on the TM1 Server and cannot be changed).

Client and group administration

These cubes assign clients to user groups and store properties for all clients on the TM1 Server.

Object attribute and properties control

These cubes store attribute and property values for objects on the TM1 Server.

Performance monitoring

TM1 lets you record basic performance statistics for clients, cubes, and servers within a series of control cubes within the TM1 Server. This feature is by default disabled and you need to enable it.

To enable this performance monitoring feature, you must be logged in as a TM1 administrator and right-click on the server where you want to enable monitoring (performance monitoring is enabled on a per-server basis) and then select **Start Performance Monitor**.

If you enable performance monitoring, TM1 populates the performance monitoring control cubes on a minute-by-minute basis. Then you can view these cubes as you would view any information stored in any other TM1 cube.

The four control cubes that hold performance statistics for clients, cubes, and servers are as follows:

- `}StatsByClient`: This cube tracks message count, average message size, total elapsed time, and other measures.
- `}StatsByCube`: This cube tracks the memory used for each cube on the server.
- `}StatsForServer`: This cube tracks the connected clients, active threads, and memory used for the server.

> The "Memory Used" statistic in this cube is not always accurate and should only be used as an estimate, because TM1 allocates memory "as it needs it" from the operating system.

- `}StatsByCubeByClient`: This cube tracks the number of cell updates, cell retrievals, view calculations, and view retrievals for each client and cube on the server.

Hold tracking by username

These cubes are used by Cognos TM1 to manage the status of individual cell called **holds**. Individual users have the ability to turn on or off this cell. Once an individual cell holds is set on, Cognos TM1 creates a control cube named `}Hold_` followed by the user ID and cube name to control the status of holds for the cube.

Cube replication

A final (but important) topic for this chapter is cube replication. Depending on your access privileges (you need to be a TM1 Admin), you can copy cubes from one server to another, and synchronize the data between the cubes. This can be done either at specified time intervals or on demand.

Replicating your cubes between your servers

Using the TM1 Replication feature, you can copy cubes and other associated objects from a remote server to your local server, or between two remote servers. This can be done by synchronizing the data bi-directionally among the copied cubes.

Replicating cubes can offer following advantages:

- Traveling "disconnected" users can update their local servers and then connect and have their cubes synchronized to the corporate database when it is convenient to them.
- The latest data can be synchronized to your laptop for "disconnected" presentations or training.
- Replication enhances the scalability of TM1.

Replication creates a relationship between two cubes and between two servers.

Replication must knows

Here are some factors about TM1 which you must know:

- **TM1 versions**: All TM1 Servers in a replication process must be the identical versions.
- **Remote servers**: You can replicate cubes that reside on only remote servers. You cannot replicate cubes that reside on other local servers.
- **Local servers**: TM1 clients can replicate cubes to their local server only if they are running that server as an independent process. The machine must have a network card. To run a local server as an independent process, clients need to select the **Local Server Execution Mode: Independent Process** option in the **TM1 Options** dialog box.
- **Access privileges**: When you replicate a source cube on a remote server to a local server, any elements to which the local client has None access on the remote server will have a value of zero. If the client has Read (or higher) access to a consolidation which includes elements to which the client has NONE access, the consolidation will appear to be the sum of only those elements to which the client has READ (or higher) access. The consolidation, as reported to the client, will not be the sum of all elements, as in the source cube.
- `Tm1s.cfg` **file**: The `Tm1s.cfg` file must be configured to register the target and source servers with the same TM1 Admin Server. If your local server wants to have its data replicated to the corporate server, your local `AdminHost` parameter must list both the corporate server and your local servers ID (separated by a semicolon).
- **Length of directory path and cube name**: The total length of the path name for the target TM1 server's data directory and the name of the cube you are replicating cannot exceed the limit of 256 characters.

- **Transaction logging**: Transaction logging must be enabled for the mirror cubes on the target server which are a part of the replication and synchronization process. If you are performing a bi-directional synchronization, transaction logging must be enabled for all the related cubes on both the source and target servers.
- **CubeProperties control cube**: The values stored in the CubeProperties control cube are specific to a TM1 Server and are not copied from the master to the target server during a replication process.
- **Dimension replication**: TM1 can be setup to replicate dimensions but by default, it does not.
- **Rule replication**: TM1 can be set up to replicate cube rules but by default, it does not.
- **Multiple server replication**: Depending on your access privileges, you can replicate a single cube on many different servers.
- **Replication of Replicated**: You can replicate a replicated cube.
- **Source cubes**: A source cube refers to **the** original cube in a replication.
- **Mirror cubes**: A mirror cube refers **to a** copy of the source cube.
- **Current replications**: The Server Explorer window lists the current replication connections beneath the **Replications** icon.
- **Source servers**: A source server is the remote server you log in to.
- **Target servers**: A target server is the server you logged in from.
- **Replication connections**: Before replicating a cube, you need to log on to a remote server and create a replication connection. This is done in Server Explorer by double-clicking on the **Replications** icon and by filling in the required information on the **Create Server Replication** dialog.

Summary

In this chapter we have discussed all of the background information pertaining to Cognos TM1 dimensions and cubes that you need to know to prepare for the current IBM Cognos TM1 Developer (Test COG-310) certification exam.

Two minute drill

Here are some key points discussed in this chapter:

- There are two ways to create cubes—by selecting dimensions from the list of existing dimensions in the **Creating Cube** window and by using TurboIntegrator to identify and map dimensions and data from an external data source to a new or existing cube.
- Each and every TM1 cube must have at least two dimensions and a maximum of 256 dimensions.
- Data is loaded into cube cells. A cell is identified by the intersection of dimensions.
- When you create a dimension, you identify the leaf-level elements that make up the dimension and, optionally, any hierarchies (consolidations) of the elements within the dimension.
- Dimension names can have a maximum of 256 characters.
- The four ways to create dimensions are by using **the Dimension Editor, TurboIntegrator, importing data into a new cube and dimension worksheets.**
- TM1 currently supports three types of elements: Numeric, consolidated, and string.
- Numeric elements can be referred to as simple element types and identify the lowest level in a dimension
- The **Dimension Element Properties** dialog is used to make property changes to the selected element.
- A hierarchy is a way to organize data at different levels of aggregation.
- The default element weight is one.
- By using dimension hierarchies, you can easily aggregate *numeric* data into categories that are meaningful in your analyses.
- If elements identify data in a cube, then think of the element attributes as describing the elements themselves.
- An alias attribute may also be used to present data in different languages!
- To create attributes and assign attribute values, you use the Attributes Editor.
- In most cases, TurboIntegrator processes will be the tool used to add, update, and delete your dimension attributes.
- When you create a dimension, an attribute named format is created for you automatically by TM1. This attribute can be used to set a display format for each individual numeric element.

- You must be a member of ADMIN to create new dimensions using the Dimension Editor window.
- A non-ADMIN user can be set up to modify an existing dimension with the Dimension Editor window.
- After creating your dimension with the Dimension Editor, you can then use it to make modifications to that dimension.
- You can copy elements from almost any source (other dimension, text file, Microsoft Excel worksheet) and paste them into the Dimension Editor to add multiple elements in one step.
- "Delete Element" removes the element from the dimension while "Delete Element from Consolidation" removes the element from its "parent element" and not from the dimension unless that element is only defined as a child of that parent.
- The order of elements in a dimension may be very important—depending upon the application! In general, you may want to order the dimensions in a cube according to their size and density (sparse and smaller dimensions should be first, followed by the more dense or larger ones).
- When you add elements to a dimension, TM1 assigns an index to each element automatically.
- You can reset the order of the elements in your dimension to determine the index value for each element in a dimension. One way to perform this is through the dimension editor.
- The way to create a cube is simple; from the TM1 Server Explorer you can just click **Cubes** | **Create New Cube** and then fill in or select the required information.
- You can always create cubes on your local server but you must be a TM1 administrator to create cubes on remote servers.
- You should always include your measures dimension as the last dimension in your cube.
- You should (try to) order your dimensions from the smallest and sparsest of dimensions to the largest and most dense dimensions.
- The order of your dimensions can impact on the performance of your cube.
- You must select at least two dimensions. The maximum number of dimensions is 256.
- Setting measures and time dimension as cube properties is not required for TM1, this feature is offered if an external OLAP client is going to access your TM1 cube as a data source.
- By default, TM1 loads all cubes into memory when a server starts.

- You can view cube and dimension characteristics in Server Explorer.
- The cubes that TM1 itself uses to perform the certain activities are called control cubes.
- All control cubes are named with a first character of } and are by default "not visible" within the TM1 Server Explorer.
- Control cubes in TM1 include security, client and group administration, object attribute and properties control, and performance monitoring.
- TM1 lets you record some basic performance statistics for clients, cubes, and servers within a series of control cubes within the TM1 Server. This is by default disabled and you need to enable it.
- You should be aware about the fact that the Memory Used statistic is not always accurate and should only be used as an estimate, because the TM1 allocates memory "as it needs it" from the operating system.
- Using the TM1 replication feature, you can copy cubes and other associated objects from a remote server to your local server, or between two remote servers. This is done by synchronizing the data bi-directionally among the copied cubes.

Self test

- **Question**: What are the two ways to create a cube?

  Response: By selecting dimensions from the list of existing dimensions in the **Creating Cube** window and by using TurboIntegrator to identify and map dimensions and data from an external data source to a new or existing cube.

- **Question**: What is the minimum number of dimensions required to create a cube?

  Response: At least two dimensions and a maximum of 256 dimensions.

- **Question**: Dimension names can have a maximum of how many characters?

  Response: A maximum of 256 characters.

- **Question**: What action should be performed on a cube prior to accumulating data in it?

  Response: Delete data from the cube.

- **Question**: When the source data contains more dimensions than the cube, which process should be used to summarize the unused data?

  Response: Accumulate.

- **Question**: What are the three ways to create dimensions?

  Response: The Dimension Editor, TurboIntegrator, and dimension worksheets.

- **Question**: What are the TM1 currently supported three types of elements?

  Response: Numeric, consolidated, and string.

- **Question**: An application developer needs to quickly populate a large number of cells in a cube with the same data. What is the fastest way to accomplish this?

  Response: Spread.

- **Question**: Why would an application developer create a lookup cube in TM1?

  Response: To reference data in another cube.

- **Question**: What type of TM1 elements can be referred to as simple element types?

  Response: Numeric elements can be referred to as simple element types and identify the lowest level in a dimension.

- **Question**: How can data be used at different levels of aggregation?

  Response: A hierarchy—by using dimension hierarchies, you can easily aggregate numeric data into categories that are meaningful in your analyses.

- **Question**: What object is the most used object to present data in multiple languages?

  Response: An alias attribute can be used to present data in multiple languages which can be created with the TM1 Attributes Editor.

- **Question**: What kind of attribute can be used to set a display format for each individual numeric element?

  Response: When you create a dimension, an attribute named format is created for you automatically by TM1. This attribute can be used to set a display format for each individual numeric element.

- **Question**: What security group must a user be to create dimensions using the TM1 Dimension Editor?

  Response: You must be a member of ADMIN to create new dimensions using the Dimension Editor window however a non-ADMIN user can be set up to modify an existing dimension with the Dimension Editor window.

- **Question**: What is the difference between "Delete Element" and "Delete Element from Consolidation"?

  Response: "Delete Element" removes the element from the dimension while "Delete Element from Consolidation" removes the element from its "parent element" and not from the dimension unless that element is only defined as a child of that parent.

- **Question**: How does TM1 keep track of elements added to a dimension?

  Response: When you add elements to a dimension, TM1 assigns an index to each element automatically.

- **Question**: What are some guidelines for creating a cube?

  Response: You should always include your measures dimension as the last dimension in your cube, you should (try to) order your dimensions from the smallest and sparsest of dimensions to the largest and most dense dimensions.

- **Question**: While creating a cube is it required for the developer to set the measures and time dimension?

  Response: Setting a measures and a time dimension as cube properties is not required for TM1, this feature is offered if an external OLAP client is going to access your TM1 cube as a data source.

- **Question**: Which cubes are automatically loaded into memory when a TM1 server starts?

  Response: By default, TM1 loads all cubes into memory when a server starts.

- **Question**: What objects does TM1 itself use to perform certain activities?

  Response: The cubes that TM1 itself uses to perform the certain activities are called control cubes.

- **Question**: How are TM1 control cubes identified?

  Response: All control cubes are named with a first character of and are by default "not visible" within the TM1 Server Explorer.

- **Question**: What are the control cubes within TM1?

  Response: The control cubes in TM1 include security, client and group administration, object attribute and properties control, and performance monitoring.

- **Question**: Does TM1 provide any way to monitor its performance?

  Response: TM1 lets you record some basic performance statistics for clients, cubes, and servers within a series of control cubes within the TM1 Server. This is by default disabled and you need to enable it.

- **Question**: What does the TM1 Replication feature allow you to do?

  Response: Using the TM1 Replication feature, you can copy cubes and other associated objects from a remote server to your local server, or between two remote servers. This can be done by synchronizing the data bi-directionally among the copied cubes.

3
TurboIntegrator (TI)

In this chapter, you will learn about the purpose and use of Cognos TM1 TurboIntegrator.

We will identify and explain the purpose and use of **TurboIntegrator** (**TI**) as well as cover the basics of using TI—focusing on the information need for the current IBM Cognos TM1 Developer (Test COG-310) certification exam.

The current certification exam assigns a weightage of 25 percent to this topic.

Introduction

TM1 TurboIntegrator is the programming or scripting tool that allows you to automate data importation, metadata management, and many other tasks.

Scripts built with TI, can be saved, edited, and, through the use of chores, be set up to run at regular intervals.

TI scripts can be used to process existing TM1 data or to import (and then process) data or information external to TM1 through the use of TI's Data Source feature.

Data sources available with TurboIntegrator

Using TurboIntegrator, you can import data from the following data sources:

- Industry standard comma-delimited (CSV) text files including ASCII files
- Information stored in relational databases (accessible through an ODBC data source)
- Other OLAP cubes, including Cognos TM1 cubes and views.
- Microsoft Analysis Services
- SAP via RFC, creating TI processes

TI's basic object is the process, which can be created by an administrator. Multiple processes can be linked together as chore objects, which allow the processes to be executed in sequence as well as to schedule processes to run for a specific time and/or interval. More recent versions of TM1 also allow processes to be called from other processes, allowing a non-sequential execution path.

To create a new TI script you can use TM1 Server Explorer. You have to just right-click on **Processes** and then select **Create New Process**. TM1 then opens the TurboIntegrator dialog showing a new, blank process ready for your code.

Within the process, there will be five visible tabs:

- The **Data Source** tab
- The **Variables** tab
- The **Maps** tab (this tab is initially grayed out)
- The **Advanced** tab
- The **Schedule** tab

You will need to know some basic information about each of the tabs in a TurboIntegrator process.

The Data Source tab

You can use the **Data Source** tab to identify the source from which you want to import data to TM1. It is also important to be aware that data sources can be programmatically defined in the **Prolog** section of the process (we will discuss this topic in *Chapter 5, Advanced Techniques for TI Scripting*).

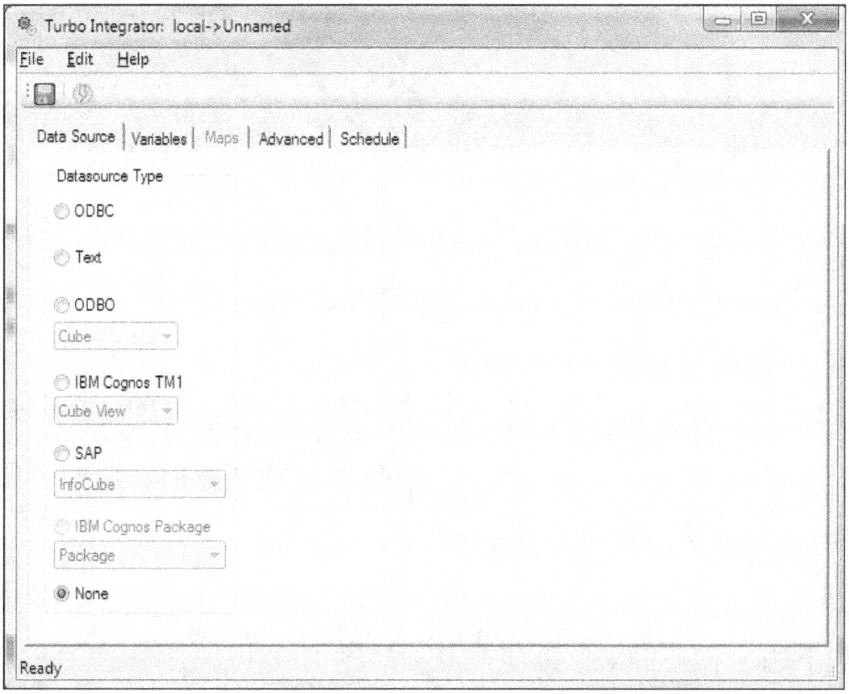

When defining a process from the TM1 Client, the path to an ASCII or ODBC data source may (and usually will) differ from the path used by the server machine that TM1 is actually running on. If this happens, the process will fail. Options for correctly dealing with this situation are covered in *Chapter 5, Advanced Techniques for TI Scripting*.

The fields and options available on the **Data Source** tab vary according to the **Datasource Type** that you select.

The Variables tab

The concept of database table columns or file fields are handled in the TI **Variables** tab. If the process has a data source defined, each column in that data source will become a variable in the **Variables** tab. Refer to the following screenshot:

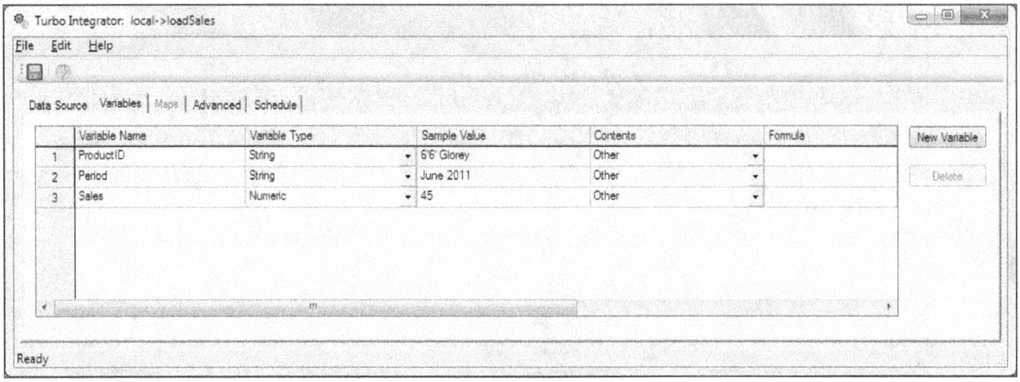

When you select (define) a data source, TM1 attempts to set up your variables in the **Variables** tab. If TI can work out what the names of the fields are, and the names are valid (that is, there are no spaces, punctuation, duplicated names, and so on) or not, it will automatically name these variables for you. If it cannot, it will give them generic names like V1, V2, V3, and so on.

> You should change these names to something more descriptive.

When TM1 processes the data, it will assign the value of each column (or field) of that row of data in the data source to the corresponding variable name. You can then use the value of the variable in processing the data.

TM1 will set you up with its best effort at defining your variables. Each variable will be listed on the **Variables** tab along with TM1's "guess" at each **Variable Type** (string or numeric). It will show the variable's purpose in the **Contents** column.

In the **Contents** column you will indicate what you want to do with the data in that variable. The options are:

- **Ignore**: If you have a variable set to **Ignore**, TI will not be able to see or use it at all and if you refer to it in any part of your code, you will get an error message when you try to save the process.

- **Element, Consolidation, Data**, or **Attribute**: These are only used when you are having TI to generate the code via the GUI. This tells TI that the contents of this variable should be one of the following:
    - An element name or a consolidation name (which TI can use to update the relevant dimension)
    - A piece of data (which TI can write into a cube)
    - An attribute (which is also used to update a dimension)
- **Other**: This is the most common selection. You will set the value to this if you want to write the code yourself.

Of course you will notice that all of your variables are listed with the contents of **Ignore**. After TM1 goes to the trouble of defining each of the variables in your data source, it promptly ignores them by setting them all with a content of **Ignore**.

The most common data content to select will be **Other**. This indicates to TM1 that this variable will be used in a function or other logic statement within that TI process.

Important facts on the **Variables** tab include:

- Be sure to verify the variable type of each and every variable. TM1 will make assumptions about your data which are not always correct. A string, which has numeric data in it, will be initially defined as numeric by TM1.
- The order of the variables in the **Variables** tab is really irrelevant to your scripting. For example, a `CellPutN` function that you code need not have variables in the same order as which appears in the variables list. The `CellPutN` function needs the variables in the order of the cube's dimensions.
- A variable is is the name of a specific value. You can use the variable's value in any way you need to; write it to a cube, use it as an element name, write it to a text file using the `ASCIIOutput` function, or whatever you want.
- TM1 will show sample data from the data source in the **Variables** tab but only if TI is currently connected to the data source.

Defining your own variables!

Although TM1 sets up the variables it sees in your selected data source, you can also define your own variables using the **New Variable** button on the **Variables** tab.

This allows you to use mathematical formulae using constant values, or the values of other variables from the defined data source. The most common use here is to use already defined variables and a business rule to create a new variable.

Keep in mind it would be just as easy as to put the business rule in script within the TI process. This will be covered in *Chapter 5, Advanced Techniques for TI Scripting*.

More on the Variables tab

Depending upon what your selected data source is, the **Variables** tab will behave a little differently. For example, if you select an existing TM1 cube as a data source, you will see in the **Variables** tab that:

- There is one variable for each of the dimensions in the selected cube
- There is one variable called **Value** which will contain the value that is stored at the intersection of the cube's dimension elements.

Local variables

When a TI process executes, a set of local variables is generated. Local variables exist only in the process in which they are used, and are not available outside of that process.

Local variables are destroyed when a process exits. These local variables include:

- `DatasourceNameForServer`
- `DatasourceNameForClient`
- `DatasourceType`
- `DatasourceUsername`
- `DatasourcePassword`
- `DatasourceCubeview`
- `DatasourceDimensionSubset`
- `DatasourceASCIIDelimiter`
- `DatasourceASCIIDecimalSeparator`
- `DatasourceASCIIThousandSeparator`
- `DatasourceASCIIQuoteCharacter`
- `DatasourceASCIIHeaderRecords`
- `Value_Is_String`
- `NValue`
- `SValue`
- `OnMinorErrorDoItemSkip`
- `MinorErrorLogMax`

- `DataSourceODBOCatalog`
- `DataSourceODBOConnectionString`
- `DataSourceODBOCubeName`
- `DataSourceODBOHierarchyName`
- `DataSourceODBOLocation`
- `DataSourceODBOProvider`
- `DataSourceODBOSAPClientID`
- `DataSourceODBOSAPClientLanguage`

Some very special local variables

TM1 provides three special variables for use:

- `NValue`: Used to access your cube data as numeric data.
- `SValue`: Used to access your cube data as a type string. Keep in mind that if the data in your cube is numeric you still have to convert it to string before using it.
- `Value_Is_String` (as a numeric value): It is `0` if the `Value` variable is numeric and `1` if it is a string (note that this refers to the value stored in the cube).

```
If (VALUE_IS_STRING=1);
  # Use CellPutS…   ..
Else;
  # Use CellPutN…
End if;
```

The Maps tab

The **Maps** tab is used if you want TM1 to generate TI code automatically for you.

For this purpose you need to perform the following steps:

1. You need to have at least one variable on the **Variables** tab.
2. The **Contents** column of the variable(s) must be set to **Element**, **Consolidation**, **Data**, or **Attribute**.

There are some additional tabs in the **Maps** tab. Two of them are described next.

Cube tab

The **Maps** tab has several additional tabs. One of them is the **Cube** tab.

Use this if you want to:

- Create (or destroy and recreate) an entire cube from the data source.
- Update the data in a cube from any variable which has a **Contents** type as **Data**.

Key points to know about the Cube tab are:

- You need to have at least two variables defined as **Element** in the **Contents** column for TI to generate code to create or recreate a cube.
- To update data in a cube you must use variables of **Contents** type **Data**.
- Generated TI code does not always follow the same syntax as that of the code written by you.
- If you select the **Recreate** option rather than the **Create** option, code will be generated to destroy the cube (if it exists) as well as to create the cube.
- You can also specify whether you want to **Store** the values or **Accumulate** the values.
- With a simple checkbox selection, cube logging can be enabled or disabled—more on cube logging later in this chapter.
- If you select **Update Cube** you can then specify the **Zero out view** to be used.

Dimensions tab

The **Dimension** tab is used if you have stated that any of your variables have an **Element** as **Contents** type. That means that the value assigned to the variable will represent the name of an element in a dimension.

The following are the key facts to know about this tab:

- The **Element Variable** column shows the name of the variable defined on the **Variables** tab.
- The **Sample Value** column is for information only.
- The **Dimension** column is dependent on the value you select for its **Action** column.
- The **Order In Cube** column only applies if you specify **Create** or **Recreate** a cube on the **Cube** tab.
- The options in the **Action** column are **Create, Recreate, Update**, and **As Is**.

- The **As Is** action will use the elements that already exist in the specified dimension. If a variable contains an element name which currently does not exist in the dimension, you will get an error when you run the process.
- The **Element Type** column indicates if the element is numeric or string.
- You can order the elements in the dimension using the **Element Order** column.

The Advanced tab

All TI processes give you the ability to provide runtime parameters. By default, a process will have no runtime parameters defined but you can insert (define) any number of parameters to be passed to your process as type of numeric or string. Refer to the following screenshot:

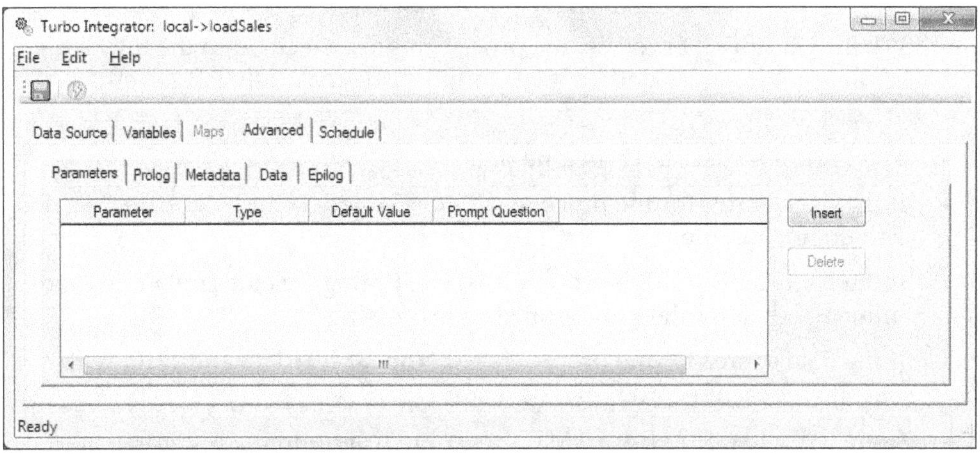

While adding parameters to a process, you can use the **Parameters** tab (under the **Advanced** tab). When you add a parameter, TM1 will name it with a **P** (for parameter) and then the next sequential number.

> Please rename your parameters to something more meaningful. Rather than **P1**, you can use something such as **PCurrentYear** or similar.

TI processes also include several procedures tabs. They are as follows:

- **Prolog**
- **Metadata**
- **Data**
- **Epilog**

These procedures can be viewed as the tabs under the **Advanced** tab in the TI editor.

Order of operations within a TurboIntegrator process

It's extremely important to be aware of and understand the following information about the tabs under the **Advanced** tab:

- When you run a TI process, the procedures are executed in the following sequence: **Prolog, Metadata**, **Data**, and **Epilog** (basically left to right as they are displayed).
- The **Prolog** is executed only one time.
- If the data source for the process is **None**; **Metadata** and **Data** are disabled and do not execute.
- If the data source for the process is **None**; **Epilog** executes only one time, immediately after the **Prolog** finishes processing.
- If the data source for the process is not **None, Metadata** and **Data** will execute for each record in the data source.
- Code to build or modify a TM1 dimension resides in the **Metadata** tab.
- The **Metadata** tab is used to build TM1 subsets.
- All lines of code in the **Metadata** procedure are sequentially executed for each record in the data source.
- All lines of code in the **Data** procedure are sequentially executed for each record in the data source.
- The **Data** procedure is executed for each row or record in the data source when an error is generated in the procedure for multiple times.
- The **Data** procedure is the procedure used to write/edit code used to load data into a cube.
- The data source is closed after the **Data** procedure is completed.
- The **Epilog** procedure is always the last procedure to be executed.

- Not all TM1 functions will work as expected in every procedure. For example, the `DimensionElementInsert` function is a TI function that can only be used in the **Data** or **Epilog** procedures of a process.

The Schedule tab

The **Schedule** tab is one of the five tabs which are visible when you open the TM1 TurboIntegrator window:

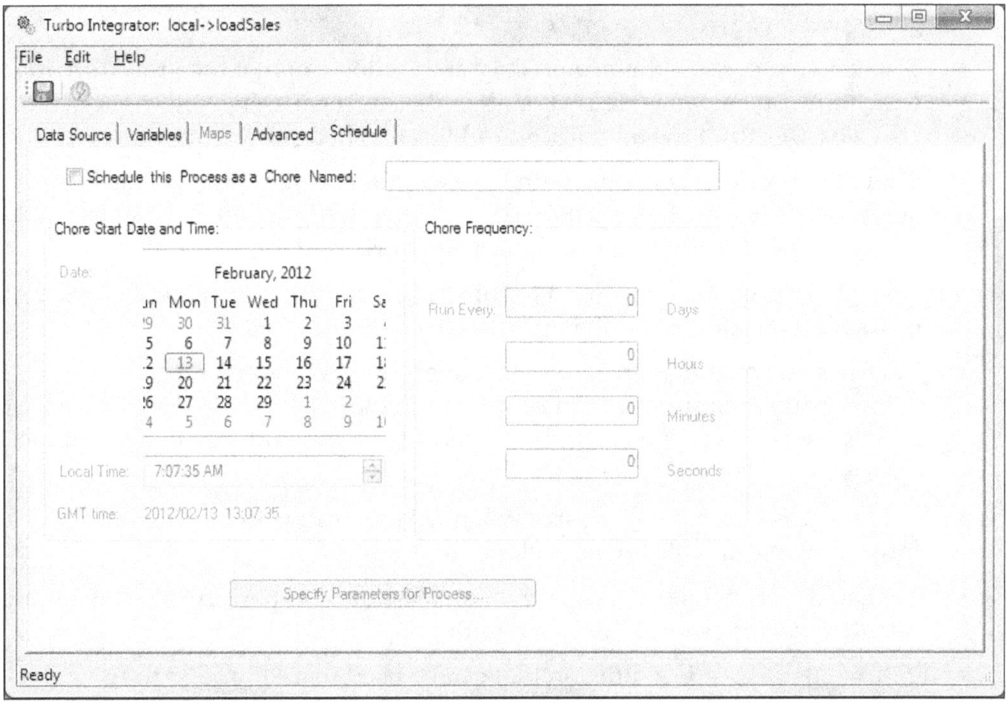

The **Schedule** tab allows you to schedule a process to execute at regular intervals. Keep the following in mind about the **Schedule** tab:

- You can use the calendar to select a start date for the process.
- Processes can be set with a frequency granularity of seconds, minutes, hours, or days.
- Parameters can be provided which are available to the process every time it runs.
- You can supply a name for the Chore that will run your process (it does not have to have the same name as the process itself).

Key notes on TurboIntegrator processes

Keep in mind the following points while creating and editing TI processes:

- A process is a TM1 object.
- **Chores** are the container objects for a set of TM1 processes. Chores allow you to run your processes in a certain order and schedule processes to be run in a certain time.
- You can modify TI generated code by copying the code present below the generated area within the process.
- TI saves changes to a dimension only at the conclusion of the procedure in which the dimension is created or altered. This means that you cannot access your changes until the tab (procedure) has finished processing.
- Both TI and Rules functions (with the exception of STET) can be used in any tab (procedure) of a process (STET is a TM1 Rules function that can be used to negate the effect of a rule and does not work in TI).
- A single TI process can be used to construct a cube view, set the view as the process's data source and then process the data in the view.
- TI writes all generated error details to the TM1 process error log. Additionally, minor errors can be written in the TM1 Message log as well, in which case a message box will be displayed showing information about the error(s).
- A TI process with no data source will have the **Prolog** and **Epilog** tabs (procedures) available for a developer to program.
- TI should be considered (rather than a TM1 Rules) to perform slow changing calculations, for example, once a month.
- `CellsUpdateable` is a function that can be used in a TI process to test a data intersection to see if the process can write to it. This can be used to avoid errors generated during runtime.
- The **Metadata** tab (procedure) is used to create new TM1 dimensions.
- To avoid hardcoded values in a TI process, parameters can be set up to pass dynamic values to the process.
- TM1 elements can (and should be) referenced by a TI instead of the element's principal name.

String lengths limit in TurboIntegrator

Remember that TI is capable of handling string data in sizes of up to 8000 bytes characters at a time. This limit applies when your TI process is performing actions such as assigning a value to a variable or importing individual records of data. Any longer record is truncated.

Reserved words

As in any programming or scripting language, TM1 utilizes a number of reserved words. If you use any of these words in your TI scripts, you will receive compile errors. There are four types of reserved words in TI:

- Rule function names such as `DATE`, `DTYPE`, and `AVG`
- Process function names such as `CellPutN` or `ASCIIOutput`
- Implicit variable names such as `DatasourceASCIIDelimiter`
- TI keywords such as `If` and `While`

Functions

TI includes a vast list of functions that you can use within the processes. In addition to these TI functions, you can also incorporate all of the TM1 Rules functions in a TI process (with the exception of the STET function).

TI functions included in the certification exam are as follows:

- `AsciiOutput`: This function writes a comma-delimited record to an ASCII file.
- `AttrPutN` and `AttrPutS`: These functions assign a value to a numeric or string element attribute.
- `CellGetN`, `CellGetS`, `CellPutN`, and `CellPutS`: These functions retrieve (or update) values from (or to) a numeric or string cube cell.
- `CellIsUpdateable`: This function lets you determine whether a cube cell can be written or not. The function returns `1` if the cell can be written, otherwise it returns `0`.
- `DimensionElementInsert` and `DimensionElementDelete`: These functions add or delete an element to or from a dimension.

- `DimensionElementComponentAdd` and `DimensionElementComponentDelete`: These functions will add or delete a component (child) to or from a consolidated element. You cannot use this function in the **Epilog** procedure of a TI process.
- `ExecuteProcess`: This function lets you execute a TI process from another process.
- `ItemSkip`: This function forces a process to skip the current data source item.
- `ItemReject`: This function rejects a source record and places it in the error log, along with a specified error message.
- `If` and `While`: The `If` statement allows a process to execute a statement or series of statements when a given expression is `true`, and `while` allows a process to repeat a series of statements when a given condition is `true`.
- `ProcessQuit`: This function terminates a TI process.
- `SecurityRefresh`: This function reads all the security control cubes and regenerates the internal structures in the server that are used by TM1 API functions.
- `SaveDataAll`: This function saves all TM1 data from the server memory to disk and restarts the log file. You should avoid using this function due to its impact on performance; instead you should enable cube logging for the cubes that are being updated.

> If enabling cube logging for the import cubes cannot be done for performance reasons, within the TM1 application there should be only one process calling the TI function called `SaveDataAll`. Use a standalone, single, distinct chore to execute the `SaveDataAll` operation.

- `SubsetCreate` and `SubsetDestroy`: These functions create or destroy a public subset of a specified dimension.
- `ViewCreate` and `ViewDestroy`: These functions create or destroy a view of a specified cube.

Cube logging

TM1 can keep a record of all data changes made to a cube. If the server stops unexpectedly, TM1 can use this logged record of changes to recover upon startup.

The logging element indicates whether logging is enabled for a given cube. When cube logging is enabled, the value of this property is `Yes`, otherwise the value is `No`.

By default, TM1 logs transactions to all cubes which are loaded on the server.

TM1 system administrators have the option to turn off logging for particular cubes.

Logging can be enabled (or disabled) from the **Security Assignments...** menu in Server Explorer (for administrators).

Care must be taken while enabling or disabling cube logging because of its potential performance impact as well as the effect on TM1 and its ability to recover from an abnormal shut down or other unexpected loss of data.

When you disable logging, TM1 accelerates the updating of the data but you cannot recover the updates in the event of a system failure.

Typically, when transactional changes are to be made to a cube, logging on that cube is enabled. If you are creating and loading a new cube, logging can be disabled.

If TI processes utilize logic that clears and reloads all data, cube logging should be turned off (disabled).

Replication requires logging enabled on replicated cubes.

Summary

In this chapter, we have discussed all of the background information pertaining to the basic mechanics and use of TM1 TurboIntegrator that you need to know to prepare for the current IBM Cognos TM1 Developer (Test COG-310) certification exam.

Two-minute drill

- TurboIntegrator is referred to as TI.
- TI can be saved, edited, and scheduled to run at regular intervals.
- TI can be used to process existing TM1 data or import and process data external to TM1.
- Using TI, you can import data from data sources such as CSV, RDBMS, TM1 Cubes, SSAS Cubes, and SAP (via RFC). Processes can be linked together and can be scheduled using chores.
- TM1 allows processes to be called from other processes.
- Within all TI processes there are five visible tabs—**Data Source**, **Variables**, **Maps**, **Advanced**, and **Schedule**.
- You can use the **Data Source** tab to identify the source from which you want to import data. The fields and options available on the **Data Source** tab vary according to the **Datasource Type** you select.
- The concept of database table columns or file fields are handled in the TI **Variables** tab.
- When you define a data source, TM1 attempts to set up your variables in the **Variables** tab.
- The most common data content to select is **Other**.
- TM1 will show sample data from the data source in the **Variables** tab but only if TI is currently connected to the data source.
- Although TM1 sets up the variables it sees in your selected data source, you can also define your own variables using the **New Variable** button in the **Variables** tab.
- Local variables exist only in the process in which they are used, and are not available outside of that process.
- Use `Value_Is_String` as a numeric value. It's `0` if the `Value` variable is numeric and `1` if it is a string.
- The **Maps** tab is used if you want TM1 to generate TI code automatically.
- Generated TI code does not always follow the same syntax as that of the code written by you.
- All TI processes give you the ability to provide runtime parameters.
- By default, a process will have zero runtime parameters but you can insert any number of parameters to be passed to your process as type of numeric or string.

- While adding parameters to a process, you can use the **Parameters** tab under the **Advanced** tab).
- When you add a parameter, TM1 will name it with a **P** (for parameter) and then the next sequential number.
- When you run a TI process, the procedures are executed in the following sequence: **Prolog**, **Metadata**, **Data**, and **Epilog** (basically left to right as they are displayed).
- **Prolog** is executed only one time.
- If the data source for the process is **None**; **Metadata** and **Data** are disabled and do not execute.
- If the data source for the process is **None**; **Epilog** executes for one time immediately after **Prolog** finishes processing.
- If the data source for the process is not **None**; **Metadata** and **Data** will execute for each record in the data source.
- Code to build or modify a TM1 dimension resides in the **Metadata** tab.
- The **Metadata** tab is used to build TM1 subsets.
- All lines of code in the **Metadata** procedure are sequentially executed for each record in the data source.
- All lines of code in the **Data** procedure are sequentially executed for each record in the data source, because the **Data** procedure is executed for each row or record in the data source in which an error generated in the procedure multiple times.
- The **Data** procedure is the procedure used to write/edit code used to load data into a cube.
- The data source is closed after the **Data** procedure is completed.
- The **Epilog** procedure is always the last procedure to be executed.
- Not all TM1 functions work as expected in every procedure.
- The **Schedule** tab allows you to schedule a process to execute at regular intervals. A process is a TM1 object.
- You can modify TI generated code by copying the code present below the generated area within the process.
- TI saves changes to a dimension only at the conclusion of the procedure in which the dimension is created or altered. This means that you cannot access your changes until the tab (procedure) has finished processing.
- Both TI and Rules functions (with the exception of STET) can be used in any tab (procedure) of a process.

- A single TI process can be used to construct a cube view, set the view as the process's data source and then process the data in the view.
- TI writes all generated error details to the TM1 process error log.
- A TI process with no data source will have the **Prolog** and **Epilog** tabs (procedures) available for a developer to program.
- TI should be considered (rather than a TM1 rule) to perform slow changing calculations, for example, once a month.
- `CellsUpdateable` is a function that can be used in a TI process to test a data intersection to see if the process can write to it. The **Metadata** tab (procedure) is used to create new TM1 dimensions.
- To avoid hardcoded values in a TI process, parameters can be set up to pass dynamic values to the process.
- As in any programming or scripting language, TM1 utilizes a number of reserved words.
- TI includes a vast list of functions which you can use within the processes. TM1 can keep a record of all data changes made to a cube. If the server stops unexpectedly, TM1 can use logged record of changes to recover upon start up.
- The `}CubeProperties` dimension is used only in the `}CubeProperties` control cube. The logging element indicates if logging is enabled for a given cube. When cube logging is enabled, the value of this property is `Yes`, otherwise the value is `No`.
- TM1 system administrators have the option to turn off logging for particular cubes.
- Care must be taken when enabling or disabling cube logging because of its potential performance impact as well as the effect on TM1 and its ability to recover from an abnormal shut down or other unexpected loss of data.
- When you disable logging, TM1 accelerates the updating of the data but you cannot recover the updates in the event of a system failure.
- Typically, when transactional changes are to be made to a cube, logging on that cube is enabled. If you are creating and loading a new cube, logging can be disabled.
- If TI processes utilize logic that clears and reloads all data, cube logging should be turned off (disabled).

Self Test

- **Question**: How can TM1 tasks be automated to run at specified intervals?

  Response: TI scripts can be saved, edited and, through the use of chores, can be set up to run at regular intervals.

- **Question**: What are the valid data sources that can be used with TI?

  Response: Industry standard comma-delimited (CSV) text files including ASCII files, information stored in relational databases (accessible through an ODBC data source, OLAP cubes, including Cognos TM1 cubes and views, Microsoft Analysis Services, and SAP.

- **Question**: How can the execution of TI scripts be controlled?

  Response: Multiple processes can be linked together with Chores, and TM1 also allows processes to be called from other processes, allowing a non-sequential execution path.

- **Question**: How are TI scripts created?

  Response: You can use TM1 Server Explorer; you just right-click on **Processes** and select **Create New Process**.

- **Question**: What are the five tabs or processes with a TI script?

  Response: The **Data Source** tab, the **Variables** tab, the **Maps** tab (this tab is initially grayed out), the **Advanced** tab, and the **Schedule** tab.

- **Question**: What is the purpose of the **Data Source** tab?

  Response: You can use the **Data Source** tab to identify the source from which you want to import data.

- **Question**: What is the purpose of the **Variables** tab?

  Response: The concept of database table columns or file fields are handled in the TI **Variables** tab. If the process has a data source defined, each column in that data source will be a variable in the **Variables** tab.

- **Question**: When you select (define) a data source, TM1 attempts to set up your variables for you in the **Variables** tab, can you change the names and settings of the variables that TM1 assigns?

  Response: Yes and you should verify each variable to ensure that they are correct.

- **Question**: What are the options for variable **Contents**?

  Response: The valid options include **Ignore, Element, Consolidation, Data, Attribute,** and **Other**.

- **Question**: What is the most common data content selected and what does it indicate?

  Response: The most common data content to select is **Other**. This indicates to TM1 that this variable is used in a function or other logic statement within that TI process.

- **Question**: True or False, TM1 shows sample data from the data source in the **Variables** tab but only if TI is currently connected to the data source.

  Response: True.

- **Question**: Why would you define your own variables within a TI process?

  Response: This allows you to use mathematical formulae using constant values, or the values of other variables from the defined data source. The most common use here is to use already defined variables and a business rule to create a new variable.

- **Question**: What are the characteristics of TI local variables?

  Response: When a TI process executes, a set of local variables is generated. Local variables exist only in the process in which they are used, and are not available outside of that process.

- **Question**: Three important local variables include `NValue`, `SValue`, and `Value_Is_String`. What are they used for within a TI process?

  Response: Use `NValue` to access your cube data as numeric data, use `SValue` to access your cube data as type string and use `Value_Is_String` to determine a values type. It's `0` if the `Value` variable is numeric and `1` if it's a string.

- **Question**: What is the purpose of the **Maps** tab?

  Response: The **Maps** tab is used if you want TM1 to generate TI code automatically for you.

- **Question**: What is required for TM1 to automatically generate TI code for you?

  Response: You need to have at least one variable on the **Variables** tab and the **Contents** column of the variable(s) must be set to **Element, Consolidation, Data,** or **Attribute**.

- **Question**: What is the purpose of the **Advanced** tab?

  Response: The **Advanced** tab is where you can provide runtime parameters to your script and insert custom program code into the sub-tabs provided.

- **Question**: What are the sub-tabs available within the **Advanced** tab of a TI process?

  Response: TI processes also include several procedures tabs. They are **Prolog, Metadata, Data,** and **Epilog.**

- **Question**: When you run a TI process, the procedures are executed in what sequence?

  Response: **Prolog, Metadata, Data,** and **Epilog** (basically left to right as they are displayed).

- **Question**: How many times does the **Prolog** tab get executed when a TI process is executed?

  Response: Only one time.

- **Question**: Code to build or modify a TM1 dimension would reside in what tab?

  Response: The **Metadata** tab.

- **Question**: What is the reason **Data** tab errors are generated multiple times?

  Response: Because the **Data** procedure is executed for each row or record in the data source when an error is generated in the procedure multiple times.

- **Question**: Code to load data into a cube is written in what tab?

  Response: The **Data** tab.

- **Question**: What is the purpose of the **Schedule** tab?

  Response: The **Schedule** tab allows you to schedule a process to execute at regular intervals.

- **Question**: How is it possible to change TI generated code?

  Response: You can modify TI generated code by copying the code below the generated area within the process.

- **Question**: When are changes made to a dimension by a TI process saved?

  Response: Only at the conclusion of the procedure in which the dimension is created or altered.

- **Question**: Where are errors generated by a TI process written?

  Response: TI writes all generated error details to the TM1 process error log.

- **Question**: For slow changing calculations, should you consider a TM1 Rules or TI process?

  Response: TI should be considered (rather than a TM1 rule) to perform slow changing calculations, for example, once a month.

- **Question**: What is the purpose of the `ItemSkip` function?

  Response: This function forces a process to skip the current data source item.

- **Question**: What is the TM1 Rules function that is not available in TI processes?

  Response: In addition to TI functions, you can also incorporate all of the TM1 Rules functions in a TI process with the exception of the STET function.

- **Question**: What is the purpose of the `SaveDataAll` function?

  Response: This function saves all TM1 data from server memory to disk and restarts the log file.

- **Question**: If enabling cube logging for the import cubes cannot be done for performance reasons, how should you use the `SaveDataAll` function?

  Response: Use a standalone, single, distinct chore to execute the `SaveDataAll` operation.

- **Question**: What is the purpose of the logging element in the `}CubeProperties` dimension?

  Response: The logging element indicates if logging is enabled for a given cube. When cube logging is enabled, the value of this property is `Yes`, otherwise the value is `No`.

- **Question**: Describe typical cube logging settings within TM1.

  Response: When transactional changes are to be made to a cube, logging on that cube is enabled. This allows recovery in case of any failure or error. If you are creating and loading a new cube, logging can be disabled. If TI processes utilize logic that clears and reloads all data, cube logging should be turned off (disabled). This is recommended to improve performance during the load.

4
Rules

In this chapter, we will review the information pertaining to Cognos TM1 Rules. It is important to understand these when taking the current IBM Cognos TM1 Developer (Test COG-310) certification exam, including the advantages of using Rules versus TurboIntegrator basic rule construction fundamentals.

The current certification exam assigns a weightage of 25 percent to the Rules topic.

Rules

One of the powers of TM1 is its native ability to quickly consolidate values defined within a dimension. Cognos TM1 Rules provides an even more powerful and flexible method to compute values within a cube. In many applications, you also need to perform calculations which do not involve aggregation, such as generating cost allocations and calculating exchange rates. You can use Cognos TM1 Rules to perform such calculations.

Additionally, rules can be written to work across dimensions and access data in other cubes.

Using TM1 Rules, you can:

- Perform multiplication of cells to calculate totals based upon business rules
- Override automatic TM1 consolidations when needed
- Use data in one cube to perform calculations in another cube or share data between cubes
- Assign the same values to multiple cells

Each and every TM1 rule is associated with an individual cube. Rules are represented as a subordinate object of the associated cube in TM1 Server Explorer. Rules only calculate values for the cubes which they are associated with.

To create a TM1 rule you can use the TM1 Rules Editor. The Rules Editor is a very simple text editor that helps you create accurate cube references, with menu options and toolbar buttons to insert commonly used rule syntax, characters, and functions.

The Cognos TM1 Rules Editor is a .NET component and therefore, to run it on your machine, you must first install the Microsoft .NET Framework 3.5 SP1. Errors will occur if you attempt to use the Rules Editor when .Net 3.5 SP1 is not properly installed.

To access the Rules Editor, you can use TM1 Server Explorer. Right-click on a cube (the cube you want to define a rule for) and from the menu select **Create Rule...** (if there are no rules already associated with this cube):

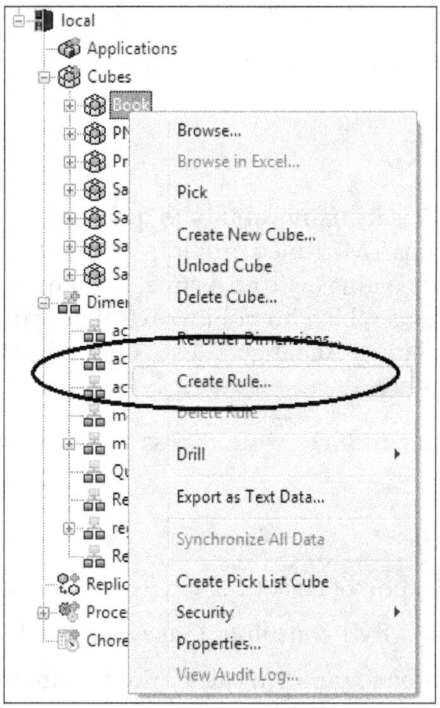

You can select **Edit Rule...** if one or more rules already exist for this cube:

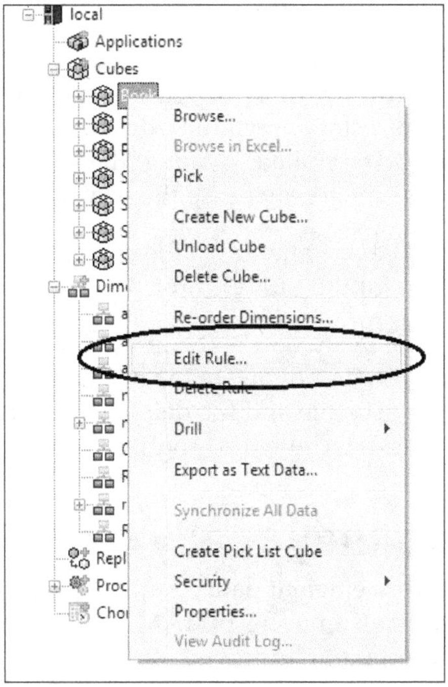

You should also be aware that, if at least one rule already exists for a cube, you can access the rule(s) by double-clicking on the rules file displayed under the cube in Server Explorer. Only one **Rules Editor** window can be opened for the same cube at a time.

TM1 rules are compiled one by one when the rules file is saved. TM1 stops compiling the rules when it encounters its first rule compile error. For example, if there are three compile errors, you would perform following steps:

1. Click on **Save**.
2. TM1 prompts for the compile error (1st error encountered).
3. Fix the error.
4. Click on **Save**.
5. TM1 prompts for the compile error (2nd error encountered).
6. Fix the error.
7. Click on **Save**.
8. TM1 prompts for the compile error (3rd error encountered).

9. Fix the error.
10. The Save operation is successful.

Successfully compiled TM1 rules are stored in files called `cube_name.rux`. When a cube for which you have defined rules is loaded into memory, TM1 searches for the cube's `.rux` file in the data directory containing the cube. If a rule file is found for the cube, the rules are loaded and compiled. Again, if there are rule compile errors, the server will encounter errors which may cause the server not to load successfully.

When you create a rule, TM1 also generates a file called `cube_name.blb`, which contains format information for the Rules Editor.

If you want to edit a `.rux` file in another text editor, you should delete the corresponding `.blb` file. If you do not delete the file, there will be a discrepancy between the contents of the `.rux` file and the display in the Rules Editor, as the display of the Rules Editor is determined by the `.blb` file.

Rules – how do they really work?

Since Cognos TM1 uses a very efficient data compression algorithm to allow large datasets to fit in relatively small amounts of RAM, TM1 calculates the values only when needed by TM1—resulting in improved performance and reduced storage requirements.

Here is the sequence of events:

1. A value is requested from (a location in) a cube.
2. TM1 Server checks if the location corresponds to the area definition of any calculation statements associated with the cube.
3. If the location does correspond to a statement, TM1 evaluates the formula portion of the calculation statement.
4. TM1 returns the calculated value to the relevant area.

It is important to know:

- Values are calculated only once for a cell
- Rules are executed with order preference and the first rule that gets applied to the cell, wins

> Multiple rules assigned to the same cell can be applied by using the `CONTINUE` function.

Like consolidations within dimensions, TM1 rules are calculated on demand. But unlike consolidations, TM1's sparse consolidation algorithm is not able to determine in advance which results will be empty without additional information. In fact, when consolidation occurs in TM1 cubes that have rules defined, the sparse consolidation algorithm is turned off. This is done to avoid incorrect results getting generated by the TM1 Rules. So when the sparse consolidation algorithm is turned off, every single cell in the cube is checked for a value during a consolidation and this can slow down cubes that are very large or sparse.

General rules of thumb:

- Remember that, if most values in your cube are zeros, this is an indication that the cube is relatively sparse.
- Multidimensional cubes are almost always sparse.
- The more dimensions a cube has, the greater is the degree of sparsity.
- In TM1, there is a distinction between a zero and a value that is missing (or non-applicable).
- In TM1, values can only be real numbers, and the value zero is used to represent zero, no (or missing) value, and even the non-applicable values.
- The impact of sparsity on calculations can be tremendous.

Sparsity

During consolidations, TM1 uses a sparse consolidation algorithm to skip over cells that contain zero or are empty. This algorithm speeds up consolidation calculations in cubes that are highly sparse. A **sparse cube** is a cube in which the number of populated cells as a percentage of total cells is low (`http://publib.boulder.ibm.com`).

Cognos TM1 provides the use of feeders to identify which cube cells need to have rules evaluated, and which can be skipped. The effective use of Cognos TM1 feeders is essential for making your rules efficient and able to avoid combinatorial explosion.

Combinatorial explosion

In mathematics, a **combinatorial explosion** describes the effect of functions that grow very rapidly as a result of combinatorial considerations.

Wikipedia

A simple example that illustrates the power of the sparse consolidation algorithm is to consider the consolidation value (8433) at the intersection of total regions and surfboard lengths. To calculate the total, you must add up every possible cell which might total 119. However, if you add only the cells with non-zero values, the number of components to add may drop down significantly.

Dissection of Cognos TM1 Rules

Cognos TM1 Rules is nothing more than calculation statements. These calculation statements define how to compute values in the cells of the cube to which the rules are assigned.

Usually, every rule you create will require one or more corresponding feeders. Feeder statements, when used correctly, ensure that the correct values are calculated by your Rules and can significantly impact on the performance of your Rules.

If you use feeder statements in a rule (and you should), the rule must also contain a `SKIPCHECK` declaration and a `FEEDERS` declaration. The `SKIPCHECK` declaration must immediately precede any calculation statements in the rule, while the `FEEDERS` declaration must precede the feeder statements.

Rules – calculation statements

A calculation statement consists of the following:

- Area definition
- Leaf, consolidation, or string qualifier
- Formula
- Terminator

Area definition

Each rule must have an area definition to define the cell values to be calculated with a rule for Cognos TM1. Using areas, you can specify which calculations apply to different parts of a cube.

For example, specific calculations may vary from region to region. So, you may need to apply different rules based upon the selected region.

Some valid area definitions include:

- `[]`: This would apply the calculation to all cells in the cube.
- `['Jan 2012']`: This would apply the calculation to all cells identified by the `Jan 2012` element.
- `['Jan 2012','New Jersey']`: This would apply the calculation to all cells identified by the `Jan 2012` and `New Jersey` elements.

- `['Jan 2012', {'New Jersey', 'New York', 'Vermont'}]`: This would identify a subset of data (by enclosing all subset members in curly braces) to apply the calculation to all cells identified by the `Jan 2012`, `New Jersey`, `New York`, and `Vermont` elements.

> The Cognos exam requires specific knowledge of how to determine rule area definitions. It would be a good idea to spend some time exercising different examples of rule area definitions.

Area definition syntax

To create a valid area definition you must:

- Enclose each element within single quotes
- Use commas to separate each element
- Enclose the entire area definition in square brackets

Special characters and non-unique element names

You can use the syntax `'dimensionname':'elementname'` to specify elements that are not unique to a single dimension or for dimension names that contain special characters.

It is important to be able to reference names which include special characters within a TM1 rule area definition. A good example is when you have to reference one of many control objects that are built into TM1. These objects contain the curly brace (}) special character. Using the previously mentioned syntax, you can write an area definition that defines the `ADMIN` group in the `Groups` dimension as follows:

```
['}Groups':'ADMIN']
```

Remember that, if an element is not unique within a cube, you must qualify the reference by adding the correct dimension name. For example, the area lets you write a statement when the element `North America` is not unique to the `Region` dimension:

```
['Units', 'Mar', 'Region':'North America']
```

The CONTINUE function and area definitions

Rules are applied sequentially. Therefore, if two rules reference the same cells defined by an area definition, the first rule encountered gets applied to the cells. You can utilize the `CONTINUE` function to apply additional rules to the cells.

Consider the following example:

```
['Mar 2011'] = 120;
['Mar 2011','Northeast'] = 0;
```

All `Mar 2011` cells would be calculated as `120` (ignoring the second rule).

Now consider if you write:

```
['Mar 2011'] = if(!Region @= 'Northeast',0,CONTINUE);['Mar 2011']=120;
```

The results are different. All cells identified by the `Mar` and `Northeast` elements are assigned a value of `0`. Cells identified by `Mar` and any other `Region` element are assigned a value of `120`.

Numeric, consolidation, or string (oh my!)

Cognos TM1 defines elements as either a numeric (`N:`), consolidation (`C:`), or string (`S:`).

The area definitions can be qualified so that TM1 knows to only apply the rule to the cells that are of the element type you have defined (the absence of any qualifier would mean that the rule calculation applies to all cell types in the area definition).

- If the qualifier is `N:`, the statement applies only to the leaf cells.
- If the qualifier is `C:`, the statement applies only to the consolidated cells.
- If the qualifier is `S:`, the statement applies only to the string cells.
- If there is no qualifier, the calculation statement applies to all cells in the defined area.

> The Cognos exam requires that you fully understand how rule qualification works! Make sure that you understand how to qualify the area of a rule to leaf level, consolidations, and so on!

TM1 rule qualifiers must immediately precede the formula component of a statement. Any qualifier placed at the start of a rule statement will cause a syntax error.

You will need to be able to interpret the following rule syntaxes:

- `['Gross Margin%']=['Gross Margin']\['Sales']*100`: No area restrictions are applied.
- `['Sales']=N:['Price']*['Units']\1000`: The calculation of `'Sales'` only applies to `N:` or leaf level elements in the cube.
- `['Sales']=C:['Sales']\['Units']*1000`: The calculation of `'Sales'` only applies to `C:` or consolidated cells.
- `['Sales']=C:['Sales']\['Units']*1000` and `N:['Price']*['Units']\1000`: There is a different calculation applied for leaf level elements and consolidated cells.

Formulas

Rule formulas can include numeric constants, arithmetic operators and parentheses, functions (those that are valid in rules), conditional logic, and references to data in other cubes.

The following sections will provide the basic information you need to know about each.

Numeric constants

There are some basic points you should know about numeric constants:

- Simplest components of a rule calculation
- Numeric
- Can include (optionally) a leading sign
- Can include (also optionally) a decimal point
- Alphabetic characters are not allowed
- Maximum length is 20 (numeric) characters
- Scientific notations are allowed

Arithmetic operators

There are some basic points you should know about arithmetic operators:

- Valid operators include signs such as plus (+), minus (-), asterisk for multiplication (*), forward slash for division (/), back slash for division which returns zero when you divide by zero (\), and caret for exponentiation (^).

- Arithmetic operators are used in the following order:
    - Exponentiation
    - Multiplication
    - Division
    - Addition
    - Subtraction
- Parentheses can be used to force a different order of evaluation.

Using conditional logic

Cognos TM1 Rules can be written to have conditional evaluation. You can use the `IF` function to force TM1 to evaluate a rule differently depending on a logic test. If you are familiar with Microsoft Excel, you will be able to recognize the format:

```
IF(Test, Value1, Value2)
```

As in Excel, if the expression `Test` is true, the rule will return `value1` otherwise the rule returns `value2`. You need to make sure that both values return the same data type or the rule will fail. TM1 does allow you to nest `IF` statements within your rule.

Along with the important `IF` function, you need to be aware of the operators you can use in TM1 for comparing values. They are (the expected) greater than (>), less than (<), greater than or equal to (>=), less than or equal to (<=), equal (=), and not equal to (<>).

To compare two string values, you must insert the @ symbol before the comparison operator.

You also need to be able to combine expressions within a TM1 rule by using the logical operators And (&), Or (%), and Not (~).

String values in Cognos TM1 can be joined (concatenated) together by using the pipe (|) character—just be sure to test the combined length of the resulting expression as TM1 only allows a single string to be up to 255 bytes.

Cube references

A very important part of understanding and using Cognos TM1 Rules is cube references which can be both internal references to data within the cube where the rule resides and external references to data within cubes other than the cube where the rule resides. Keep in mind that you can only write rules which reference data in a cube that resides on the same TM1 Server.

To reference data in another cube, you must use the `DB` function. The `DB` function returns a value from a cube in a TM1 database. It returns a numeric value if used in a numeric expression and a string value if used in a string expression.

Just keep in mind that internal cube references use the same syntax as the area definitions.

External cube references

To reference data in a cube other than the cube where the rule resides, you need to code the `DB` function. The `DB` function must reference the cube (where the data you want to retrieve lives) and then a value for each of the dimensions in that cube:

```
DB('Cube', dimension value, dimension value,... dimension value)
```

In the default TM1 Rules Editor, you can click on the button labeled **DB(...)** to insert a DB rule to reference another TM1 cube:

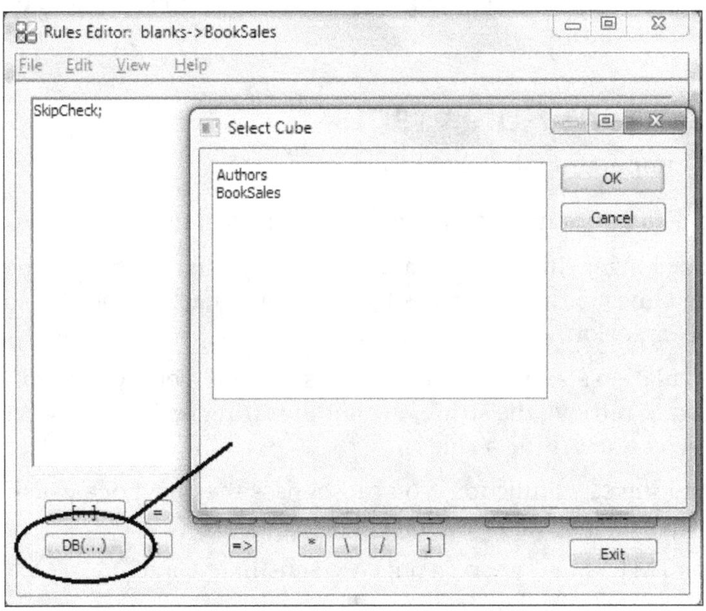

Your dimension value can be a value that exists in the referenced dimension (within single quotes), the name of the dimension preceded by an exclamation point (which indicates the value currently being requested), or even an expression that evaluates the value within the referenced dimension.

The DB function can be extremely useful when referencing data in a lookup cube implemented in the system such as a currency rate cube and the DB function can be used multiple times within a TM1 rule. This is referred to as nested DB functions. Remember, with nested DB functions, you must ensure that the inner DB function returns a valid argument to the outer DB function:

```
['Gross Sales','Budget']=N:
  IF(!Period@='2012',
    IF(!Customer@='00001001',
      DB('BookSales',!Customer,'Gross Sales','Prior','Actuals'),
        DB('BookSales',!Customer,'Gross Sales','Current','Actuals')
        ),
      STET);
```

The Cognos exam specifically references the DB function and its use.

Drill assignment rule

Cognos TM1 allows you to create a link between two cubes that have related data. To do this, you have to create a drill assignment rule. Keep in mind that this type of rule must be defined as a string.

More important Rules facts

There are some important facts about Rules:

- You must use a semicolon to end every rule statement.
- To make longer rules more readable, you can distribute statements over multiple lines in the cube rules file, as long as each of the statements ends with a semicolon.
- If a calculation statement references a string element, you must use a DB function to retrieve the string, even if the string resides in the same cube for which you are writing a rule.
- By using the STET function, you can bypass the effect of a calculation statement for specific areas of a cube.
- Cognos TM1 Rules syntax is not case-sensitive.
- You can use spaces within rules to improve clarity.

- A rules statement can occupy one or more lines in the Rules Editor. It can also contain one or more formulas. End each statement with a semicolon.
- To add comments and to exclude statements from processing, insert the number (#) sign at the beginning of a line or statement
- The length of a comment line is limited to 255 bytes. For comments longer than 255 bytes, you must break up the comment into multiple lines, with each one including the number sign (#) at the beginning.
- When more than one statement in a set of rules is applied to the same area, the first statement takes precedence.
- The exclamation point (or bang) can be used in a rule to evaluate to the current element of a referenced dimension.
- If you reference any object containing a special character in TM1 Rules, the object name must be enclosed in single quotation marks.
- If a calculation must be updated continuously (in real time), you should create a rule for it, conversely, if a calculation is slow moving—say updated only one time per month, it would be a better idea to utilize a **TurboIntegrator** (**TI**) process to maintain the data.
- You can load a rule file using a TI process by using the `RuleLoadFromFile` function.

Rules performance

Cognos TM1 Rules is very powerful but not always the best way to calculate results. For example, although it is possible to write rule logic to calculate consolidations within dimensions, dimension calculations work automatically and are therefore always faster than a rule. The subject of performance is a topic that is beyond this chapter but should not be overlooked.

Key notes on Rules behaviors

There are some important points about behaviors of Rules:

- Cognos TM1 Rules takes precedence over dimension consolidations but keep in mind that if a rule refers to cells in the cube that are the result of a consolidation calculation, the calculation is performed first, then the rule is calculated based upon that result. Going the other way, if a consolidation calculation is based upon cells that are the result of a rule, the rule will execute first and then the consolidation.

- You have no control over the order in which Cognos TM1 performs dimension consolidations. So, do not write rules that override consolidated elements.
- Cognos TM1 allows you to apply more than one rule to a cube cell. This is called **rule stacking** and is only limited to the machine memory. TM1 calculates the cell value based upon how the rule statements are coded.
- It is important to understand the precedence of Cognos TM1 Rules. For example, if you create a rule to apply to all elements in a dimension but do not see the results you expected, you will need to determine if a rule exists above or before the rule that affects this area.
- Again, as in Microsoft Excel, circular references are not allowed within Cognos TM1 Rules.
- You also need to be aware of how TM1 deals with percentages and fractions. Depending upon your requirements for precision you may have to rethink your rule logic.
- It is not uncommon for a rule to be written to move data from one level to another (leaf or `N:` level to a consolidation).
- Typical functions used in Cognos TM1 Rules include `DIMIX`, `DIMNM`, `DNEXT`, `TIMVL`, and `STET`.
- If a calculation occurs naturally in a dimension (hierarchy) consolidation, use it! Do not write a rule to circumvent the fast consolidation engine!

Rule feeders

The more rules you implement the more overall cube performance will be impacted. Specifically, the native consolidation ability of TM1 will slow down. To address this performance issue, you must make use of the `SKIPCHECK` and `FEEDERS` declarations.

Adding rules to a cube will impact TM1's ability to utilize its sparse consolidation algorithm. Fortunately, you can tell TM1 where to look for rules-derived values.

The `SKIPCHECK` declaration should be placed in the cube's rule file. This turns on the TM1 sparse consolidation algorithm.

[The Cognos exam requires full understanding of `SKIPCHECK`!]

The `FEEDERS` declaration indicates that you have provided feeder statements which will ensure that the correct cells are not skipped during consolidations.

Each feeder statement must have a feeder area and a reference to a rules-calculated value.

Whenever a feeder statement identifies a rules-derived value, which is a non-zero value, a placeholder is fed to the cells defined on the right-hand side of the feeder statement. This forces TM1 to include these rules-derived values when performing its consolidations.

To illustrate the need for feeders, we can consider a simple example. Suppose you have implemented rules within a cube and notice that period leaf elements such as the individual months, all have values but the consolidations for quarter and year show zero value. This is a simple example but it indicates the visual cue that one or more feeders are needed in the cube.

Another declaration to be aware of is the `FEEDSTRINGS` declaration. This must be used if any of your rules define string values. This will ensure that string values are fed properly (in the same manner as described above for the `FEEDERS` declaration).

You should try to make your rules as specific as possible—meaning that the area definition of each rule should be as explicit and specific as possible. If this is not possible you can specify a larger area and this is known as **overfeeding**. Overfeeding can be used to ensure correct values within the cube but be aware that it may also significantly impact overall performance. The opposite of overfeeding is of course underfeeding. This is when you fail to feed cells that contain rules-derived values and this will result in incorrect data.

Persistent feeders

To improve the reload time of cubes with feeders, set the `PersistingOfFeeders` configuration parameter to true (`T`) to store the calculated feeders to a feeders file. Any installation with a server load time of over five minutes can probably improve its performance using this parameter.

When this parameter is set to `T` and the server encounters a persistent feeder file, it loads the saved feeders which reduces the time normally taken to recalculate those feeders. Feeders are saved when the data is saved or rules are edited. You do not explicitly save the feeders.

For installations with many complex feeder calculations persisting feeders , re-loading feeders at server startup will improve performance. For simple feeders, the time taken to read feeders from disk may exceed the time to re-calculate the feeders but most installations will get benefit from this.

Using the persistent feeders feature will increase your system size on disk only. Memory size is not affected by the use of this parameter.

The special feeders

You can edit the Cognos TM1 configuration file to add the parameter `PersistingOfFeeders=T`. When this parameter is set and a cube with rules is saved, the feeders are stored alongside the cube data in a `.feeders` file. The cube files are called `cube-name.cub` and `cube-name.feeders`. This `.feeders` file will be used by TM1 to reload the feeders for the cube rather than taking the time to re-evaluate the actual feeders in the cube.

These `.feeders` files may be deleted from the data directory to force a complete re-calculation of feeders when the next server starts. The best way is to use a TI process and the `DeleteAllPersistentFeeders()` function to delete all persistent feeders. TM1 will monitor the modified time of the `.feeders` file and if the related cube file is newer than the feeders file, TM1 will delete and recreate the `.feeders` file.

Modifying rules and feeders

Once a feeder is loaded into memory it never gets deleted, even if the rule that the feeder is associated with has been modified or deleted, rendering the feeder invalid. Additionally, if you are using persistent feeders (described above) and if TM1 recreates a feeders file, it will include all of the feeders for the cube that are in memory so these invalid feeders are included within the new persistent feeders file. To resolve this, you will have to re-calculate all of your feeders periodically by using the `DeleteAllPersistentFeeders()` function (within a TI process) and then restarting the TM1 Server.

Guidelines for simple feeders

There are some important guidelines for simple feeders:

- Every calculation statement in a rule should have a corresponding feeder statement.
- The simplest feeders are those that apply to calculations within one dimension of one cube, where the presence of a non-zero value in one element implies the presence of a non-zero value in another element.
- To write accurate feeders, you need to focus on which component(s) of a formula determines when a non-zero value is returned to the area.
- Formatting errors within a rules file will cause a rules file to become corrupted.
- Do not attempt to edit the rules file of a cube using a non-TM1 editor.
- When working with inter-cube rules, calculation statements reside in the target cube, while feeder statements always reside in the source cube.

- TM1 feeders are used in parallel with TM1 rules to reduce the number of calculations done by the rules.
- Feeders are not required to make rules work. However, they can yield dramatic performance improvements in sparse cubes.

Troubleshooting

To diagnose rule issues, you can utilize the Cognos TM1 Rules Tracer. The Rules Tracer will allow you to:

- Trace feeders, to ensure that selected leaf cells are feeding rules-calculated cells properly
- Check feeders, to ensure that the children of a selected consolidated cell are fed properly as well as verifying that the calculation paths of the selected cells are correct

A practical example for using the Rules Tracer is in the event that you notice a rules-calculated consolidation is not calculating correctly. In this case, you would first review the consolidation's children to ensure that they are being fed properly. The easiest way to do this is to utilize the Check Feeders feature of the Rules Tracer.

Rules Tracer

There are some key facts about Rules Tracer:

- The Rules Tracer functionality is available only in the Cube Viewer.
- Rules Tracer lets you trace the way a selected cell feeds other rules-calculated cells.
- Because you can only feed from a leaf element, this option is not available for consolidated cells. The option is, however, available for leaf cells defined by the rules.
- The Rules Tracer window contains two panes.
- The Rules Tracer window's top pane displays the definition of the current cell location, as well as the feeder statements associated with the current cell.
- The Rules Tracer window's bottom pane displays the locations fed by the current cell.
- If a cube has a rule attached that uses `SKIPCHECK` and `FEEDERS` declarations, you can use Rules Tracer to check that the components of consolidations which are subject to rules are properly fed.
- You can check feeders only from a consolidated cell.

- You can trace the calculation path of all cube cells that are derived from either rules or consolidation. These cells appear shaded in the Cube Viewer.
- Tracing a calculation path can help you determine if the value for a cell location is being calculated properly.
- Rules Tracer lets you trace the way a selected cell feeds other cells.
- Since you can only feed from a leaf element, this option is not available for consolidated cells. The option is, however, available for cells defined by the rules.

Summary

In this chapter, we have discussed all of the background information pertaining to Cognos TM1 Rules that you need to know to prepare for the current IBM Cognos TM1 Developer (Test COG-310) certification exam.

Two minute drill

- One of the powers of TM1 is its native ability to quickly consolidate values defined within a dimension. You can use TM1 Rules to perform simple to complicated calculations.
- Using TM1 Rules, you can perform the multiplication of cells to calculate totals based upon business rules.
- Using TM1 Rules, you can override automatic TM1 consolidations when needed.
- Using TM1 Rules, you can use data in one cube to perform calculations in another cube, or share data between cubes.
- Using TM1 Rules, you can assign the same values to multiple cells.
- Each and every TM1 rule is associated with an individual cube.
- To create a TM1 rule you can use the TM1 Rules Editor.
- The Rules Editor is a very simple text editor.
- Cognos TM1 Rules Editor is a .NET component and therefore, to run it on your machine you must first install the Microsoft .NET 3.0 framework.
- Successfully compiled TM1 rules are stored in files called `cube_name.rux`.
- When you create a rule, TM1 also generates a file called `cube_name.blb`, which contains format information for the Rules Editor.
- It is important to know that values are calculated for a cell only once.

- Rules are executed with order preference and the first rule that applies to the cell wins.
- Multiple rules assigned to the same cell can be applied by using the CONTINUE function.
- In TM1, there is a distinction between a zero and a value that is missing (or non-applicable).
- In TM1, values can only be real numbers and the value zero is used to represent zero, no (or missing) value, and even the non-applicable values.
- Cognos TM1 provides the use of feeders to identify which cube cells need to be rules-evaluated, and which can be skipped.
- Usually, every rule you create will require one or more corresponding feeder.
- Feeder statements, when used correctly, ensure that correct values are calculated by your rules and can significantly impact on the performance of your rules.
- If you use feeder statements in a rule, the rule must also contain a `SKIPCHECK` declaration and a `FEEDERS` declaration.
- A calculation statement consists of an area definition, leaf, consolidation, or string qualifier, formula, and a terminator.
- Each rule must have an area definition to define which cell values to calculate with a rule for Cognos TM1.
- To create a valid area definition you must enclose each element within single quotes, use commas to separate each element, and enclose the entire area definition in square brackets.
- You can use the syntax `'dimensionname':'elementname'` to specify elements that are not unique to a single dimension or for dimension names which contain special characters.
- Rules are applied sequentially.
- You can utilize the `CONTINUE` function to apply additional rules to the cells.
- Cognos TM1 defines elements as either a numeric (`N:`), consolidation (`C:`), or a string (`S:`).
- TM1 rule qualifiers must immediately precede the formula component of a statement.
- The rule formulas can include numeric constants, arithmetic operators and parentheses, functions (those that are valid in Rules), conditional logic, and references to data in other cubes.

- Numeric constants are the simplest components of rule calculation statements.
- Arithmetic operators can be used in the following order:
    - Exponentiation
    - Multiplication
    - Division
    - Addition
    - Subtraction
- Parentheses can be used to force a different order for arithmetic operators during evaluation.
- To compare two string values, you must insert the @ symbol before the comparison operator.
- String values in Cognos TM1 can be joined (concatenated) together by using the pipe (|) character—just be sure to test the combined length of the resulting expression as TM1 allows a single string to be only up to 254 bytes.
- To reference data in another cube you must user the `DB` function. The `DB` function returns a value from a cube in a TM1 database.
- You must use a semicolon to end every rule statement.
- The length of a comment line is limited to 255 bytes. For comments longer than 255 bytes, you must break up the comment into multiple lines, with each one including the number sign (#) at the beginning.
- The exclamation point (or bang) can be used in a rule to evaluate the current element of a referenced dimension.
- Typical functions used in Cognos TM1 rules include `DIMIX`, `DIMNM`, `DNEXT`, `TIMVL`, and `STET`.
- The `SKIPCHECK` declaration should be placed in the cube's rule file. This turns on the TM1 sparse consolidation algorithm.
- To improve the reload time of cubes with feeders, set the `PersistingOfFeeders` configuration parameter to true (`T`) to store the calculated feeders to a `.feeders` file. Any installation with a server load time of over five minutes can probably improve its performance using this parameter.
- When working with intercube rules, calculation statements reside in the target cube, while feeder statements always reside in the source cube.
- Rules Tracer functionality is available only in the Cube Viewer.

- Rules Tracer lets you trace the way a selected cell feeds other rules-calculated cells.

Self test

- **Question**: What is one of the native powers of TM1?

  Response: Its native ability to quickly consolidate the values defined within a dimension.

- **Question**: What are the four most important abilities that TM1 Rules provides?

  Response: The four abilities that TM1 Rules provides are as follows:

  - Perform the multiplication of cells to calculate totals based upon business rules
  - Override automatic TM1 consolidations when needed
  - Use data in one cube to perform calculations in another cube or share data between cubes
  - Assign the same values to multiple cells

- **Question**: How are Cognos TM1 rules represented?

  Response: Rules are represented as a separate icon below the associated cube in TM1 Server Explorer.

- **Question**: What tool would one use to create a rule?

  Response: To create a TM1 rule you can use TM1 Rules Editor. The Rules Editor is a very simple text editor.

- **Question**: Where are TM1 rules stored?

  Response: Successfully compiled TM1 rules are stored in the files called `cube_name.rux`. When a cube for which you have defined rules is loaded into memory, TM1 searches for the cube's `.rux` file in the data directory containing the cube. If a rule file is found for the cube, the rules are loaded and compiled.

- **Question**: How often are cell values calculated within TM1?

  Response: Values are calculated for a cell only once.

- **Question**: What occurs when TM1's sparse consolidation algorithm is turned off?

  Response: When the sparse consolidation algorithm is turned off, every single cell in the cube is checked for a value during a consolidation and this can slow down cubes that are very large or sparse.

- **Question**: Name some indications that are detected if a cube is sparse.

  Response: If most values in your cube are zeros, this is an indication that the cube is relatively sparse.

- **Question**: Give a definition of a TM1 rule.

  Response: TM1 rules are nothing more than calculation statements. These calculation statements define how to compute values in cells of the cube that the rules are assigned to.

- **Question**: What are the components of a TM1 rule?

  Response: An area definition, leaf, consolidation, or string qualifier, formula, and a terminator.

- **Question**: What is the purpose of a rule area definition?

  Response: Each rule must have an area definition to define which cell values to calculate with a rule for Cognos TM1. Using areas you can specify which calculations to apply to different parts of a cube.

- **Question**: What should be done to create a valid area definition?

  Response: Enclose each element within single quotes, use commas to separate each element, and enclose the entire area definition in square brackets.

- **Question**: How do you handle non-unique references within a TM1 rule?

  Response: You can use the syntax `'dimensionname':'elementname'` to specify elements that are not unique to a single dimension or for dimension names that contain special characters.

- **Question**: Rules are applied sequentially. Therefore, if two rules reference the same cell defined by an area definition, the first rule encountered gets applied to the cell. How can you apply additional rule logic to these cells?

  Response: You can utilize the `CONTINUE` function to apply additional rules to the cells.

- **Question**: What are the three types of elements defined by TM1?

  Response: Cognos TM1 defines elements as either a numeric (`N:`), consolidation (`C:`), or a string (`S:`).

- **Question**: What is the maximum length of a numeric constant?

  Response: The maximum length of a numeric constant is 20 (numeric) characters.

- **Question**: Can you force a different order of arithmetic operators for evaluation in a TM1 rule?

  Response: Parentheses can be used to force a different order of arithmetic operators' evaluation within a TM1 rule.

- **Question**: How can one define string values within a Cognos TM1 rule?

  Response: You must insert the @ symbol before the comparison operator.

- **Question**: How do you reference data in another cube in a TM1 rule?

  Response: To reference data in another cube, you must use the `DB` function. The `DB` function returns a value from a cube in a TM1 database. It returns a numeric value if used in a numeric expression and a string value if used in a string expression.

- **Question**: What type of rule do you need to define for a drill assignment rule?

  Response: Cognos TM1 allows you to create a link between two cubes that have related data. To do this, you can create a drill assignment rule. Keep in mind that this type of rule must be defined as a string.

- **Question**: How is the end of a rule indicated?

  Response: You must use a semicolon to end every rule statement.

- **Question**: What is the purpose of the `STET` statement?

  Response: By using the `STET` function, you can bypass the effect of a calculation statement for specific areas of a cube.

- **Question**: What is the exclamation point or bang in respect to Cognos TM1 Rules?

  Response: The exclamation point (or bang) can be used in a rule to evaluate the current element of a referenced dimension.

- **Question**: How can you reference TM1 object names that contain special characters?

  Response: If you reference any object containing a special character in TM1 rules, the object name must be enclosed in single quotation marks.

- **Question**: Define rule stacking.

  Response: Cognos TM1 allows more than one rule to be applied to a cube cell. This is called rule stacking and is only limited by machine memory. TM1 calculates the cell value based upon how the rule statements are coded.

- **Question**: What is the purpose of the `SKIPCHECK` declaration?

  Response: The `SKIPCHECK` declaration should be placed in the cube's rule file. This turns on the TM1 sparse consolidation algorithm.

- **Question**: What does the `FEEDERS` declaration indicate?

  Response: The `FEEDERS` declaration indicates that you have provided feeder statements that will ensure that the correct cells are not skipped during consolidations.

- **Question**: Name the requirements of a feeder statement.

  Response: Each feeder statement must have a feeder area and a reference to a rules-calculated value.

- **Question**: Does each rule require a feeder?

  Response: Every calculation statement in a rule should have a corresponding feeder statement.

- **Question**: What should you focus on when writing feeders?

  Response: To write accurate feeders, you need to focus on which component(s) of a formula determines whether a non-zero value is returned to the area or not.

- **Question**: When working with intercube rules, where should the rules and the corresponding feeders reside?

  Response: Calculation statements reside in the target cube, while feeder statements always reside in the source cube.

- **Question**: Must a rule have a feeder to work?

  Response: Feeders are not required to make rules work. However, they can yield dramatic performance improvements in sparse cubes.

- **Question**: How can you determine if rules you created for a cube are being fed correctly?

  Response: If a cube has a rule attached that uses the `SKIPCHECK` and `FEEDERS` declarations, you can use Rules Tracer to check that the components of consolidations that are subject to rules are properly fed.

5

Advanced Techniques for TI Scripting

In this chapter, we will discuss advanced techniques for **TurboIntegrator** (**TI**) scripting in regards to the current IBM Cognos TM1 Developer (Test COG-310) certification exam.

Specifically, we will review the advanced tabs in TI and how they are used, the differences between the four TI scripts, we will identify where to apply custom scripts, and finally we will also provide some tips and tricks you can use when creating TI.

The current certification exam assigns a weightage of 10 percent to this topic.

ETL

Most applications built with Cognos TM1 require some way to perform data **ETL** which is an acronym for extract, transform, and load. It is a process that involves extracting data from an outside source, transforming it into some form to fit an operational need, and then loading that newly formatted data into a target.

Cognos TM1 provides TI to meet this requirement. TurboIntegrator or TI gives you the power to develop a process that can recognize an outside data source, pull and transform that data, and then load it into TM1. These processes that you create can be saved and scheduled to run as needed.

In *Chapter 3, TurboIntegrator (TI)*, we covered the basic or fundamental workings of TI and what you need to know to do well when taking the current certification exam. In this chapter, we will reaffirm some of these basics as well as drill deeper into some of the more advanced areas of TI scripting—as it relates to the current certification exam.

TM1 TurboIntergrator review

TM1 TurboIntegrator is the programming or scripting tool that allows you to automate data importation, metadata management, and many other tasks.

Scripts built with TI can be saved, edited and, through the use of chores, be set up to run at regular intervals.

TI scripts can be used to process existing TM1 data or, through the use of TI's Data Source feature, import (and then process) data or information external to TM1.

Within each process there are six sections or tabs. They are as follows:

- **Data Source**
- **Variables**
- **Maps**
- **Advanced**
- **Schedule**

The Data Source tab

You use the **Data Source** tab to identify the source from which you want to import data to TM1.

When defining a process from the TM1 Client, the path to an ASCII or ODBC data source may (and usually will) differ from the path used by the server machine that TM1 is actually running on. If this happens, the process will fail.

The fields and options available on the **Data Source** tab vary according to the **Datasource Type** that you select. Refer to the following screenshot:

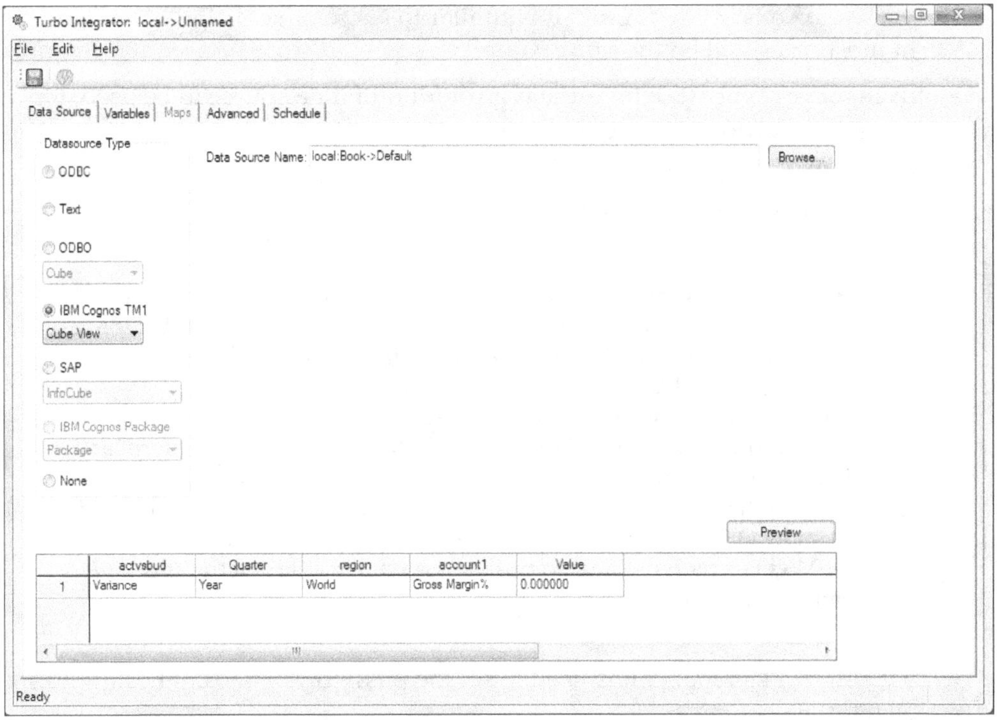

In *Chapter 3, TurboIntegrator (TI)* we mentioned the ability to programmatically define a data source as well as options to avoid errors caused by a change in the location of a defined data source. Let us get into the details of that now.

One of the steps of creating a TI process is to select **Datasource Type**. For example, a common task for a TI process is to read a text file of data and load it into a Cognos TM1 cube. To accomplish this, you select **Datasource Type** as **Text** and then use the **Browse...** button under the **Data Source** tab to locate your file. This is a simple step when you first develop your process. Browse to the file, click on **Preview** and see the data. From there you can define your variables, and so on. As previously mentioned, the specific path of the file (for example, `C:\program files\test data\TM1Data\myfile.txt`) may change or become invalid for a variety of reasons. To avoid this problem it is best to programmatically define your data source. To do this, (and to do well in the certification exam) you will need to know the following TM1 TurboIntegrator local variables:

- `DatasourceNameForServer`: This variable lets us set the name of the data source to be used. This value can (and should) include a fully qualified path or other specific information that qualifies your data source. For example, a TM1 Server's server name, cube name, and so on.

- `DatasourceNameForClient`: It is similar to `DatasourceNameForServer` and in most cases will be the same value.
- `DatasourceType`: It defines the type or kind of data source to be used, for example, view or character delimited.
- `DatasourceUsername`: When connecting to an ODBC data source, this is the name used to connect to the data source.

> In computing, **Open Database Connectivity** (**ODBC**) is a standard software interface for accessing **database management systems** (**DBMS**). The designers of ODBC aimed to make it independent of programming languages, database systems, and operating systems. Thus, any application can use ODBC to query data from a database, regardless of the platform it is on or DBMS it uses. ODBC accomplishes platform and language independence by using an ODBC driver as a translation layer between the application and the DBMS. The application thus only needs to know ODBC syntax, and the driver can then pass the query to the DBMS in its native format, returning the data in a format the application can understand—Wikipedia.

- `DatasourcePassword`: It is used to set the password when connecting to an ODBC data source.
- `DatasourceQuery`: It is used to set the query or SQL string used when connecting to an ODBC data source.
- `DatasourcecubeView`: It is used to set the name of the cube view when reading from a TM1 cube view. This can be the name of an existing cube view or a view that the process itself defines.
- `DatasourceDimensionsubset`: It is used to set the name of the subset when reading from a TM1 subset. This can be the name of an existing subset or a subset that the process itself defines.
- `DatasourceASCIIDelimiter`: This can be used to set the ASCII character to be used as a field delimiter when `DatasourceType` is character delimited.
- `DatasourceASCIIDecimalSeperator`: This TI local variable sets the decimal separator to be used in any conversion from a string to a number or a number to a string.
- `DatasourceASCIIThousandSeperator`: This TI local variable sets the thousands separator to be used in any conversion from a string to a number or a number to a string.
- `DatasourceASCIIQuoteCharacter`: This TI local variable sets the ASCII character used to enclose the fields of the source file when `DatasourceType` is character delimited.

- DatasourceASCIIHeaderRecords: It specifies the number of records to be skipped before processing the data source.

Two additional variables to be aware of are:

- OnMinorErrorDoItemSkip: This TI local variable instructs TI to skip to the next record when a minor error is encountered while processing a record. This variable is useful in scenarios where a single bad field/value in a record causes multiple minor errors.
- MinorErrorLogMax: This TI local variable defines the number of minor errors that will be written to the TM1ProcessError.log file during process execution. If this variable is not defined in the process, the default number of minor errors written to the log file is 1000.

Using TurboIntegrator Variables

To the point, an example of using these variables would be to read the input file name and the location of that file from a TM1 cube defined for this purpose. An information cube may be defined with two dimensions—application name and application measure. These two dimensions can be used to define a data point in a cube for specific applications to store and retrieve specific information, such as in the following example. Therefore, a TI process would read a file name to be loaded and the location of that file to be loaded:

```
datasourcePath = CellGetS(NameOfInformationCubeName,
MeasureNameForCategoryMeasureNameForFilePathName );
dataFileName = CellGetS( InformationCubeName, MeasureNameForCategory,
MeasureNameForFileName) ;
```

Additionally, the process may also read a location to write exceptions or errors that may occur during the processing:

```
exceptionFilePath =  CellGetS( systemVariableCubeName,
systemVariableCategory , systemVariableLogsFileName ) ;
```

Then, we can build our exception variable:

```
exceptionFileName = exceptionFilePath | 'my process name' |_
Exceptions.txt';
```

Of course, it is always a good practice to make sure that exception files are cleaned up before this process begins. So, in the process' prolog we code:

```
# --- Delete the exception file for this run so that it may be created
fresh
ASCIIDelete(exceptionFileName);
```

Finally, we use some of the previously mentioned process variables to actually set up our data source (and in this example we are using an ASCII text file as a data source):

```
# --- set the datasource info for this process
DatasourceNameForServer = datasourcePath | dataFileName;
DataSourceType = 'CHARACTERDELIMITED';
DatasourceASCIIDelimiter = ',';
```

Using the above technique, a process can run without any changes required in any TM1 environment of instance, assuming of course that the same cube is defined in all environments and is loaded with the appropriate file names, directory paths, and locations.

Dynamic Definitions

Another advanced technique is to programmatically define a view in a TI process and then set that process' data source to that view name. It is not that uncommon to define a `View` to zero-out cells in a cube to which the process will load incoming data, but it is little more interesting to define a view which will be read as input by the process itself. Let's look at an example of this.

First, the following code can be used to define a subset:

```
# ---Define cube/dimensions.
companyDimName = 'BalanceSheet Company';
# ---Define temporary subsets/view names
tempSubsetName = 'tempSubset_BS_CompareToPriorDayActual';
tempViewName = 'tempView_BS_CompareToPriorDayActual';
# --- create the subset on the company dimension
SubsetCreate(companyDimName,tempSubsetName);
SubsetElementInsert(companyDimName,tempSubsetName, allCompany,1);
# --- Setup source view
ViewCreate(cubeName,tempViewName);
ViewSubsetAssign(cubeName,tempViewName,companyDimName,
tempSubsetName);
ViewExtractSkipCalcsSet(cubeName,tempViewName,0);
ViewExtractSkipZeroesSet(cubeName,tempViewName,1);
ViewExtractSkipRuleValuesSet (cubeName, tempViewName, 1);
```

Finally, set the data source of our TI process to the temporary view name:

```
# Initialize view
DatasourceNameForServer= cubeName;
DataSourceType='VIEW';
DatasourceCubeview = tempViewName;
```

> A trick to remember here is when you first create the process, you can manually create the subset and view, select it as your data source, and let TM1 fill in your variables. After you have saved these changes, you can delete the subset and view and use the programmatic approach shown above to create the view each time the process is executed.

Recall that the epilog section of a TI process is executed once at the very end of the process execution. Therefore, in the epilog of your process you can then write the code to clean-up the subset and view (you must always destroy the view first):

```
# Cleanup view
ViewDestroy(cubeName, tempViewName);
```

Then destroy the subset:

```
SubsetDestroy(companyDimName, tempSubsetName);
```

Another good habit to get into is to check for the existence of a view or subset before attempting to create it:

Use the following lines to check for the existence of a subset or view with the same name that may already exist on the dimension or cube you are using:

```
SubsetExists(DimName, SubsetName);
ViewExists(CubeName, ViewName);
```

These functions will return `0` if the subset or view name does not already exist. If these functions return `1`, you know that a subset or view with that name already exists on the dimension or cube which will allow you to avoid a TI error.

Important TurboIntegrator functions

The following section describes some of the most important Cognos TM1 TurboIntegrator functions.

ExecuteProcess

Another advanced (and handy) feature to be aware of is the TurboIntegrator `ExecuteProcess` function. This is a very useful function. It allows you to execute a TI process from within a TI process. Obviously, you cannot have a process call itself.

The format is as follows:

```
ExecuteProcess(ProcessName, [ParamName1, ParamValue1,
ParamName2, ParamValue2]);
```

The function will return a real value that you should always test for an acceptable return code value (and do something appropriate based upon this value).

The most important return values to know are as follows:

- `ProcessExitNormal()`: If your `ExcuteProcess` returns this, it indicates that the process executed normally.
- `ProcessExitMinorError()`: If your `ExcuteProcess` returns this, it indicates that the process executed successfully but encountered minor errors.
- `ProcessExitByQuit()`: If your `ExcuteProcess` returns this, it indicates that the process exited because of an explicit `quit` command.
- `ProcessExitWithMessage()`: If your `ExcuteProcess` returns this, it indicates that the process exited normally, with a message written to `Tm1smsg.log`.
- `ProcessExitSeriousError()`: If your `ExcuteProcess` returns this, it indicates that the process exited because of a serious error.

A very simple example of using `ExecuteProcess` and checking the return code value would be:

```
returnvalue = ExecuteProcess('load_surfboard_daily_sales');
if(returnvalue = ProcessExitSeriousError() )
  ASCIIOutput(ExcpetionFile, sSeriousErrorMsg);
endif;
```

ItemSkip

The `ItemSkip` function can be used to skip a record or row of data. Keep in mind that it is very important to account for all records of data read from any data source. So, be very careful when using this function.

Usually, the function includes some type of conditional logic when it is used:

```
If (record_is_invalid);
  ASCIIOutput (exceptionFile, recordId);
  ItemSkip;
Endif;
```

ProcessBreak, ProcessError, and ProcessQuit

It is worth mentioning the following functions available in TI:

- `ProcessBreak`
- `ProcessError`
- `ProcessQuit`

These processes are important because they can be used to:

- Stop all processing and force control to the epilog
- Terminate a process immediately
- Terminate a process immediately with errors

View handling

In this section, we will look at the various functions for view handling.

ViewZeroOut

This function sets all data points (all cells) in a named view to zero. It is most often used after defining a very specific view. For example, suppose that you want to clear all data for the year 2011 in a cube named `Sales`. An example would be to create a subset on the `Period` dimension with one element in it—`2011`—and then to create a view on the `Sales` cube and assign that `Period` subset to it. Finally, perform `ViewZeroOut` on this view as shown in the following code snippet:

```
DimName = 'Period';
Cube = 'Sales';
ViewName = 'SampleView';
subName = 'SampleSubset';
```

```
SubsetCreate(DimName, SubName);
SubsetElementInsert(DimName, SubName, '2011', 1);
ViewCreate(Cube, ViewName);
ViewSubsetAssign(Cube, ViewName, DimName, SubName);
ViewZeroOut(Cube, ViewName);
```

PublishView

This function is provided to publish a private view to the TM1 Server so that other TM1 Clients can see and use the view. This was not possible in early versions of TM1 unless you were a TM1 Administrator. The format of this function is:

```
PublishView(Cube, View, PublishPrivateSubsets, OverwriteExistingView);
```

The arguments (parameters) passed to the function are extremely important!

The `PublishPrivateSubets` function determines if any private subsets that are part of the view should be made public with the view. If you say no and there are private subsets, the function will fail and the view will not be published.

`OverWriteExistingView` determines if the function can overwrite an existing public view with the same name or not. Be careful with this one—if you say yes (overwrite), you may accidentally overwrite a public view that just happens to have the same name. If you say no (do not overwrite) and there is an existing view with the same name, the function will fail and the view will not be published.

CubeClearData

The importance of this function is simply that if you want to clear the entire cube, this function is extremely fast. You could also accomplish this by building a view and performing `ViewZeroOut`—but again, keep in mind that this function is much more efficient.

CellIsUpdateable

This is an important function. You can use this to avoid runtime TI generated errors but when using it before each cell insert the following lines:

```
If (CellsUpdateable(CubeName, DimName1, DimName2, DimName3=1);
  CellPutN(myValue, CubeName, DimName1, DimName2, DimName3);
Else;
  ASCIIOuput(ExcpetionFile, RecordID, ErrorMsg);
Endif;
```

SaveDataAll

This is a very important function!

Since Cognos TM1 is an in-memory database, it keeps all of the data and changes to that data in the machine's memory and actually saves the changes to the hard disk at specific times, such as when TM1 Server is shut down. If the server crashes before TM1 is successfully shut down, active data changes in memory may be lost.

This function saves all TM1 data from the server memory to disk and restarts the log file—IBM.

To avoid this problem, you can use the `SaveDataAll` function. However, it is important to use this function appropriately. This function used incorrectly can cause server locks and crashes.

SubsetGetSize

`SubsetGetSize` is a useful function that returns a count of the total elements that are in a given subset. Here is an example of using this function to initialize a loop.

First we establish the number of elements in the subset named as `mySubsetName` and then using a counter named as `iLoopCounter`, we loop through all of the elements in the subset, retrieve the name of each element, and write that name to an output file as shown in the following code snippet:

```
iTotalElements = SubsetGetSize(myDimName, mySubsetName);
iLoopCounter = 1;
While (iLoopCounter <= iTotalElements);
  sElementName = SubsetGetElementName(myDimName, mySubsetName,
ElementIndex);
  ASCIIOutput(exceptionFile, sElementName;
  iLoopCounter = iLoopCounter + 1;
End;
```

Security functions

TM1 provides specific functions to set up and maintain TM1 security. You should be aware of the following functions before taking the certification exam:

- `AddClient` and `DeleteClient`: The `AddClient` function creates and the `DeleteClient` function deletes the clients on the TM1 Server. These functions must be used in the metadata section of a TI process.

- `AddGroup` and `DeleteGroup`: The `AddGroup` function creates and the `DeleteGroup` function deletes the groups on the TM1 Server. These functions must be used in the metadata section of the TI process.
- `AssignClientToGroup` and `RemoveClientFromGroup`: The `AssignClientToGroup` function will assign and the `RemoveClientFromGroup` will remove an existing client from an existing group.
- `ElementSecurityGet` and `ElementSecurityPut`: The `ElementSecurityGet` function is used to assign and the `ElementSecurityPut` function is used to retrieve a security level for an existing group for a specific dimension element. The security levels can be None, Read, Write, Reserve, Lock, and Admin.
- `SecurityRefresh`: The `SecurityRefresh` function reads all of the currently set up TM1 security information and applies that information to all of the TM1 objects on the TM1 Server. Be advised, depending on the complexity of the TM1 model and the security that has been set up, this function may take a very long time to execute and during this time all users are locked.

Rules and feeders Management functions

The following three functions can be used to maintain cube rules and feeders. They are important to be familiar with:

- `CubeProcessFeeders`
- `DeleteAllPersistantFeeders`
- `ForceSkipCheck`
- `RuleLoadFromFile`

CubeProcessFeeders

This function becomes important if you are using conditional feeders. Whenever you edit and save a cube rule file, feeders get automatically reprocessed by TM1. However, when you use conditional feeders certain changes to data may not cause all of the conditional feeders to be reprocessed. You can use this function to ensure that all of the conditional feeders are reprocessed. Keep in mind that all of the feeders for the cube will be reprocessed:

```
CubeProcessFeeders(CubeName);
```

DeleteAllPersistentFeeders

Recall from an earlier chapter that to improve performance you can define feeders as persistent. TM1 then saves these feeders into a `.feeder` file. These feeder files will persist (remain) until they are physically removed. You can use the `DeleteAllPersistentFeeders` function to clean up these files.

ForceSkipCheck

This function can be placed in the prolog section of a TI process to force TM1 to perform as if the cube to which the process is querying has `SkipCheck` in its rules—meaning it will only see cells with values rather than every single cell.

RuleLoadFromFile

This function will load a cube's rule file from a properly formatted text file. If a rule file exists for the named cube, it will be overwritten with the new one. If no rule file exists for the cube, TM1 will create a rule file for the named cube from the file being loaded.

Remember to be sure that the file is formatted according to the TM1 Rules conventions (you can review the format of rules in *Chapter 4, Rules*). You cannot supply a file name when you use this function but you must supply a cube name. If you leave the text file argument empty, TI looks for a source file with the same name as the cube (but with a `.rux` extension) in the server's data directory.

```
RuleLoadFromFile(Cube, TextFileName);
```

SubsetCreateByMDX

We have discussed building subsets using the `SubsetCreate` and `SubsetElementInsert` functions earlier in this chapter. Another method that can be used to create a subset is by using the `SubsetCreateByMDX` function. This function creates a subset based upon a properly formatted MDX expression.

MDX is a powerful way to create complicated lists. However, TM1 only supports a small number of MDX functions (not the complete MDX list). You will find that different versions of TM1 support different functions. Before using MDX in TM1 you need to check under **Reference Material | MDX Function Support** in the main help file supplied with the version of TM1 you are using. If TM1 encounters an unsupported MDX function, you will receive the message **Failed to compile expression**.

Another issue with MDX created subsets is that it may change based upon data changes and the resulting subset may even be an empty subset.

The format of this function is as follows:

```
SubsetCreatebyMDX(SubName, MDX_Expression);
ExecuteCommand
```

This is a function that you can use to execute a command line. The great thing about this is that you can do all sorts of clever things from within a TI process. The most useful is to execute an external script or MS Windows command file. The format of this function is as follows:

```
ExecuteCommand(CommandLine, Wait);
```

`CommandLine` is the command line you want to execute and the `Wait` parameter will be set to either `1` or `0` to indicate if the process should wait for the command to complete before proceeding.

It is strongly recommended that you allow the process to continue and not wait for the command to complete to avoid locking the TM1 Server if the external command fails or encounters a deadlock condition of its own.

Additionally, do not use this function to call any external process that logs back into the same TM1 Server. This will result in a possible deadlock scenario.

Order of operations within a TurboIntegrator process

As we have mentioned in *Chapter 4, Rules,* it is extremely important to be aware of and understand the following information about the sub-tabs of the **Advanced** tab:

- When you run a TI process, the procedures are executed in the following sequence (basically left to right as they are displayed):
    - **Prolog**
    - **Metadata**
    - **Data**
    - **Epilog**
- **Prolog** is executed one time only.
- If the data source for the process is **None, Metadata** and **Data** are disabled and do not execute.

- If the data source for the process is **None**, **Epilog** executes one time immediately after **Prolog** finishes processing.
- If the data source for the process is not **None**, **Metadata** and **Data** will execute for each record in the data source.
- Code to build or modify a TM1 dimension resides in the **Metadata** tab.
- The **Metadata** tab is used to build TM1 subsets.
- All lines of code in the metadata procedure are sequentially executed for each record in the data source.
- All lines of code in the data procedure are sequentially executed for each record in the data source.
- Because the data procedure is executed for each row or record in the data source, an error is generated in the procedure for multiple times.
- The data procedure is the procedure used to write/edit code used to load data into a cube.
- The data source is closed after the data procedure is completed.
- The epilog procedure is always the last procedure to be executed.
- Not all TM1 functions will work as expected in every procedure.

Aliases in TurboIntegrator functions

In *Chapter 4, Rules* we learned that you can use aliases to reference a dimension element in your TI process. Let us look at a practical example. Let us suppose that a company does forecasting on a monthly basis. Each month a new version of the working forecast is created. For example, in January the forecast consists of 12 months of forecasted sales (January through December). In February, the working forecast consists of one month (January) of actual sales data and 11 months of forecasted sales (February through December). In March, the working forecast consists of two months (January and February) of actual sales and 10 months of forecasted sales—and so on. In this example, you can define an alias attribute on the version dimension and use it to refer to whatever version of the forecast is currently running (or is the working version).

Then, TI processes can refer to a version as the working forecast (the alias) and always connect to the correct version.

More on data sources

It is important to understand the practical uses of a data source in a TI function. For example, it is common to define versions of views (say a forecast) and then perform operations with them. Let us look at an example. If a TM1 model utilized a reporting cube and each month the working version needed to be copied to that cube, a developer could easily define a view of the working forecast and set up a simple TI process to use that view as its data source to copy (write) it to the reporting cube.

CubeSetLogChanges

In TI, you can turn on (or turn off) cube logging using the function `CubeSetLogChanges`. Be very careful to understand when and why to turn on (or off) cube logging. If data changes are to be made to a cube with your TI process and you need to ensure that you can recover those changes in the event of a server crash, you need to assure that logging is on. If it is not important to recover changes made by the TI process, set cube logging off to improve performance. For example, copying a version of a forecast from a source cube to a reporting cube may be an example where cube logging is not important:

```
CubeName = 'SalesReporting';
SetLoggingOnFlag = 1;
SetLoggingOffFlag = 0;
CubeSetLogChanges(CubeName, SetLogginOnFlag);
```

Or

```
CubeName = 'SalesReporting';
SetLoggingOnFlag = 1;
SetLoggingOffFlag = 0;
CubeSetLogChanges(CubeName, SetLoggingOffFlag);
```

Revisiting variable types

In the **Contents** column of the TurboIntegrator **Variables** tab you indicate what you want to do with the data in that variable. The options are:

- **Ignore**: If you have a variable set to **Ignore**, TI will not be able to see or use it at all and if you refer to it in any part of your code, you will get an error message when you try to save the process.

- **Element, Consolidation, Data**, or **Attribute**: These are only used when you are having TI to generate the code via the GUI. This tells TI that the contents of this variable should be one of the following:
    - An element name or consolidation name (which TI can use to update the relevant dimension)
    - A piece of data, which TI can write into a cube
    - An attribute, which is also used to update a dimension
- **Other**: This is the most common selection. You will set the value to this if you want to write the code yourself.

TurboIntegrator sections

Each of the sections or tabs in a TI process can be referred to as a script and have a unique purpose. For example, the metadata section (or script) can be used to create and maintain TM1 dimension objects. The metadata script can also be utilized to create and maintain subsets.

TI processes can also have no data source defined. In this case, only the prolog and the epilog sections are available to you.

It is also important to fully understand that the code in the metadata and data sections will execute for each record or row in the defined data source.

The Data section (or script) is the section that is used to perform `CellPut` operations to actually load data from the data source into a cube.

Summary

In this chapter, we have discussed some of the more advanced Cognos TM1 TurboIntegrator scripting techniques that you will need to know and be comfortable with before taking the current IBM Cognos TM1 Developer (Test COG-310) certification exam. We have also looked at some practical examples.

Two minute drill

There are some important points you should know:

- The current certification exam assigns a weightage of 10 percent to the Advanced Techniques for TI Scripting topic.
- ETL is an acronym for extract, transform, and load.
- TM1 TurboIntegrator is the programming or scripting tool that allows you to automate data importation, metadata management, and many other tasks.
- Scripts built with TI, can be saved, edited and, through the use of chores, be set up to run at regular intervals.
- TI scripts can be used to process existing TM1 data or, through the use of TI's Data Source feature, import (and then process) data or information external to TM1.
- Within each process there are six sections or tabs. They are:
    - **Data Source**
    - **Variables**
    - **Maps**
    - **Advanced**
    - **Schedule**
- You can use the **Data Source** tab to identify the source from which you want to import data to TM1.
- The fields and options available on the **Data Source** tab vary according to the **Datasource Type** that you select.
- You need to know the following TM1 TurboIntegrator local variables:
    - `DatasourceNameForServer`
    - `DatasourceNameForClient`
    - `DatasourceType`
    - `DatasourceUsername`
    - `DatasourcePassword`
    - `DatasourceQuery`
    - `DatasourcecubeView`
    - `DatasourceDimensionsubset`
    - `DatasourceASCIIDelimiter`

  - `DatasourceASCIIDecimalSeperator`
  - `DatasourceASCIIThousandSeperator`
  - `DatasourceASCIIQuoteCharacter`
  - `DatasourceASCIIHeaderRecords`

- `DatasourceNameForServer` lets us set the name of the data source to be used.
- `DatasourceType` sets the type or kind of data source to be used, for example, view or character delimited.
- `DatasourceUsername` is the name to be used to connect to the data source when connecting to an ODBC data source.
- `DatasourcecubeView` is used to set the name of the cube view when reading from a TM1 cube view.
- `DatasourceDimensionSubset` is used to set the name of the subset when reading from a TM1 subset.
- `DatasourceASCIIDelimiter` can be used to set the ASCII character to be used as a field delimiter when the `DatasourceType` is character delimited.
- `DatasourceASCIIDecimalSeperator` is a TI local variable that sets the decimal separator to be used in any conversion from a string to a number or a number to a string.
- `DatasourceASCIIThousandSeperator` is a TI local variable that sets the thousands separator to be used in any conversion from a string to a number or a number to a string.
- `DatasourceASCIIQuoteCharacter` is a TI local variable that sets the ASCII character used to enclose the fields of the source file when `DatasourceType` is character delimited.
- The `DatasourceASCIIHeaderRecords` variable specifies the number of records to be skipped before processing the data source.
- An advanced technique is to programmatically define a view in a TI process.
- A trick to remember is when you first create the process you can manually create the subset and view, select it as your data source, and let TM1 fill in your variables. After you have saved these changes you can delete the subset and view and use the programmatic approach shown above to create the view each time the process is executed.
- Another advanced (and handy) feature to be aware of is the TurboIntegrator `ExecuteProcess` function. This function allows you to execute a TI process from within a TI process.

- `ProcessExitNormal()` will be returned from the `ExecuteProcess` function to indicate that the process executed normally.
- `ViewZeroOut` will set all data points (all cells) in a named view to zero.
- `CubeClearData` is a function that will clear an entire cube, and this function is extremely fast.
- `SaveDataAll` saves all TM1 data from server memory to disk and restarts the log file.
- `subsetGetSize` is a useful function that returns a count of the total elements that are in a given subset.
- `PublishView` is provided to publish a private view to the TM1 Server so that other TM1 Clients can see and use the view.
- `PublishPrivateSubsets` determines if any private subsets that are part of the view should be made public with the view.
- `OverWriteExistingView` determines if the function can overwrite an existing public view with the same name or not.
- TM1 provides specific functions to set up and maintain TM1 security.
- The `AddClient` function will create and the `DeleteClient` function will delete clients on the TM1 Server.
- The `AddGroup` function will create and the `DeleteGroup` function will delete groups on the TM1 Server.
- The `AssignClientToGroup` function will assign and the `RemoveClientFromGroup` function will remove an existing client to an existing group.
- The `ElementSecurityGet` function will assign and `ElementSecurityPut` will retrieve a security level for an existing group for a specific dimension element.
- The `SecurityRefresh` function reads all of the currently set up TM1 security and applies that information to all of the TM1 objects on the TM1 Server.
- `CubeProcessFeeders` becomes important if you are using conditional feeders.
- The `RuleLoadFromFile` function will load a cube's rule file from a properly formatted text file.
- `SubsetCreateByMDX` will create a subset based upon a properly formatted MDX expression.
- MDX is a powerful way to create complicated lists; however, TM1 only supports a small number of MDX functions (not the complete MDX list).

- `ExecuteCommand` can be used to execute a command line.
- When you run a TI process, the procedures are executed in the following sequence—**Prolog**, **Metadata**, **Data**, and **Epilog** (basically left to right as they are displayed).
- Code to build or modify a TM1 dimension resides in the **Metadata** tab.
- The **Metadata** tab is used to build TM1 subsets.
- All lines of code in the metadata procedure are sequentially executed for each record in the data source.
- All lines of code in the data procedure are sequentially executed for each record in the data source because the data procedure is executed for each row or record in the data source for which an error generated in the procedure for multiple times.
- In TI, you can turn on (or turn off) the cube logging using the function `CubeSetLogChanges`.
- In the **Contents** column of the **Variables** tab, you will indicate what you want to do with the data in that variable.
- Each of the sections or tabs in a TI process can be referred to as a script and has a unique purpose.
- TI processes can also have no data source defined. In this case, only the prolog and the epilog sections are available to you.
- It is also important to fully understand that the code in the metadata and data sections will execute for each record or row in the defined data source.
- The data section (or script) is the section that is used to perform `CellPut` operations to actually load data from the data source into a cube.

Self-Test

- **Question**: What is one of the native powers of TM1?

  Response: Its native ability is to quickly consolidate values defined within a dimension.

- **Question**: What is ETL?

  Response: ETL is an acronym for extract, transform, and load.

- **Question**: What does TM1 provide to do ETL?

  Response: Cognos TM1 provides TI to meet this requirement.

- **Question**: What is TurboIntegrator?

  Response: TM1 TurboIntegrator is the programming or scripting tool that allows you to automate data importation, metadata management, and many other tasks.

- **Question**: Within each process there are six sections or tabs. What are they?

  Response: They are **Data Source**, **Variables**, **Maps**, **Advanced**, and **Schedule**.

- **Question**: What do you use the **Data Source** tab for?

  Response: You use the **Data Source** tab to identify the source from which you want to import data to TM1.

- **Question**: What is the `DatasourceNameForServer` variable used for?

  Response: This variable lets us set the name of the data source to be used.

- **Question**: What is the **Datasource Type** used for?

  Response: It sets the type or kind of data source to be used, for example, view or character delimited.

- **Question**: What is the `DatasourceUsername` used for?

  Response: When connecting to an ODBC data source, this is the name to be used to connect to the data source.

- **Question**: What is the `DatasourcecubeView` variable used for?

  Response: This variable is used to set the name of the cube view when reading from a TM1 cube view. This can be the name of an existing cube view or a view that the process itself will be defining.

- **Question**: What is the `DatasourceDimensionSubset` variable used for?

  Response: This is used to set the name of the subset when reading from a TM1 subset.

- **Question**: What is the `DatasourceASCIIDelimiter` variable used for?

  Response: This can be used to set the ASCII character to be used as a field delimiter when the `DatasourceType` is character delimited.

- **Question**: What is the `DatasourceASCIIQuoteCharacter` variable used for?

  Response: This TI local variable sets the ASCII character used to enclose the fields of the source file when `DatasourceType` is character delimited.

- **Question**: What is the `DatasourceASCIIHeaderRecords` variable used for?

  Response: It is used to indicate the number of records to be skipped before processing the data source.

- **Question**: Where would you most likely implement code to clean-up a subset or view?

  Response: Recall that the epilog section of a TI process is executed once at the very end of the process execution. Therefore, in the epilog of your process you can then write the code to clean up the subset and view.

- **Question**: Describe the purpose of the `ExecuteProcess` function.

  Response: Another advanced (and handy) feature to be aware of is the TurboIntegrator `ExecuteProcess` function. This is a very useful function. This function allows you to execute a TI process from within a TI process. Obviously, you cannot have a process call itself.

- **Question**: What is the `ItemSkip` function used for?

  Response: The `ItemSkip` function can be used to skip a record or row of data.

- **Question**: What is the `ViewZeroOut` function used for?

  Response: This function will set all data points (all cells) in a named view to zero.

- **Question**: What is the `SaveDataAll` function used for?

  Response: This function saves all TM1 data from server memory to disk and restarts the log file.

- **Question**: What is the purpose of the `PublishView` function?

  Response: This function is provided to publish a private view to the TM1 Server so that other TM1 Clients can see and use the view.

- **Question**: What is the purpose of the `AddClient` and `DeleteClient` functions?

  Response: The `AddClient` function creates and the `DeleteClient` function deletes the clients on the TM1 Server.

- **Question**: What is the purpose of the `AddGroup` and `DeleteGroup` functions?

  Response: The `AddGroup` function creates and the `DeleteGroup` function deletes the groups on the TM1 Server.

- **Question**: What is the purpose of the `AssignClientToGroup` and `RemoveClientFromGroup` functions?

  Response: The `AssignClientToGroup` function will assign and the `RemoveClientFromGroup` will remove an existing client to an existing group.

- **Question**: What is the purpose of the `ElementSecurityGet` and `ElementSecurityPut` functions?

  Response: The `ElementSecurityGet` function is used to assign and the `ElementSecurityGet` function is used to retrieve a security level for an existing group for a specific dimension element.

- **Question**: What is the meaning of the `ProcessExitNormal()` variable?

  Response: If your `ExcuteProcess` returns this it indicates that the process executed normally.

- **Question**: What does the `SecurityRefresh` function do?

  Response: The `SecurityRefresh` function reads all of the currently set up TM1 security and applies that information to all of the TM1 objects on the TM1 Server.

- **Question**: What are the functions that can be used to maintain cube rules and feeders?

  Response: The following three functions can be used to maintain cube rules and feeders and are important to be familiar with:

    - `CubeProcessFeeders`
    - `DeleteAllPersistantFeeders`
    - `RuleLoadFromFile`

- **Question**: What does the `RuleLoadFromFile` function do?

  Response: This function loads a cube's rule file from a properly formatted text file.

- **Question**: What does the `ExecuteCommand` function do?

  Response: This is a function that you can use to execute a command line.

6 Drill-through

In this chapter, we will discuss the Cognos TM1 drill-through functionality with regards to the current IBM Cognos TM1 Developer (Test COG-310) certification exam. We will go over what it is, how it works, and how to construct an application with drill-through capabilities.

The current certification exam assigns a weightage of 5 percent to this topic.

What is drill-through?

Drill-through can be described as the act of exploring related information. Also, this can be described as the act of moving between related data via a link of some kind. Most specifically, drill-through usually exploits a relationship between master and detail information. By clicking on a master item in the master information, the details of the clicked or selected item are then displayed or otherwise made available.

Drill-through is a very important feature supported out of the box by Cognos TM1. Out of the box, functionality is referring to abilities or features that the default install of Cognos TM1 provides. This functionality provides business value with little or no custom programming or development effort required.

Components of TM1 drill-through

It is actually pretty straightforward to implement drill-through in TM1. You have to simply use one (or more) drill TurboIntegrator (TI) process (or processes) and one (or more) drill rule (or rules) to associate a data intersection point (a cell) with detailed or related data. It is important to understand that the related data or information can be detailed data, or really any other relevant information that you choose.

The two components that make up the drill-through feature in Cognos TM1 are:

- **Drill process**: The drill processes that you create will define the detailed or related data that you want to assign to the drill-from data intersection point (the drill-from cell).
- **Drill assignment rule**: The drill assignment rules that you create will define the relationship between the drill-from and the drill-to.

Once you have created the drill-through, TI processes, and drill assignment rules, you can execute that process (by right-clicking on the drill-from cell) and open the detail (or associated) information in a new TM1 Cube Viewer window.

Where to drill from?

Typically you set up a drill-through with the intention of drilling from a cell in a view in an Open Cube Viewer.

> Keep in mind that you can also drill from a view which is displayed in an Excel Slice as well as from an Active Form. We will give more details on this later in this chapter.

Drill-through (source) types

There are basically three types of supported drill-through types—meaning that there are three ways to source your drill-to data:

- TM1 cube views
- ODBC
- Other

TM1 cube views

This type of drill-through is drilling from an originating TM1 cube view to any other cube view of data. You can literally drill-through to any saved or dynamically defined cube view as long as it resides on the same TM1 Server as the originating cube view.

You can define cube views that actually exceed the maximum amount of memory that Cognos TM1 can allocate when you access a view.

> Remember, by default, this memory threshold (`MaximumViewSize`) is a parameter in the `TM1s.cfg` file. This default is 100 MB (on a 32-bit system) and 500 MB on a 64-bit system.

MaximumViewSize

This is an optional parameter. It sets the maximum size that a cube view can display. This is any cube view—not just a drilled-to cube view. You do not have to stop and restart the TM1 Server for this parameter change to take place—it is set when the `.cfg` file is saved. If you do not set this parameter and the defaults (100 or 500 MB) are exceeded, TM1 will display an error message.

The Format is as follows:

```
MaximumViewSize=n
```

Where n represents the amount of memory in MB to be allocated.

> Remember from *Chapter 1, The Components of TM1* that the TM1 configuration (`.cfg`) file is a simple text file that can be accessed and updated using a simple text editor such as Windows Notepad.

ODBC

You can define a drill-through from an originating cube to any valid ODBC source as long as the ODBC source being drilled to is accessible from the computer on which the TM1 Server is running.

Some examples of valid ODBC sources would include:

- dBase files
- Microsoft Excel worksheets
- MS Access databases
- Relational databases such as Microsoft SQL Server

Other

Keep in mind that you can implement a drill-through from any TM1 cube view to any data source supported by TI.

Now, let us look at the basics of implementing a very simple drill-through in Cognos TM1.

Drill process

Drill processes are simply TI processes that you create or define in a different way than the method of creating and saving TI processes described earlier in this book.

A drill-through process is used to define the detailed or related data (the data that will ultimately be displayed or opened in a new window). The TM1 cube, that is, the source (displays the master or original data, or where the drill-through originates) is known as or is referred to as the origination cube.

Another way to think about a drill process is that it is the Cognos TM1 object that is used to specify the connection information in a drill-through.

> It is very important to be familiar with the data that originates the drill-through as well as the data that your drill-through will be drilling to (or the data that will be displayed in a new window).

Creating a drill process

A drill process can be created by performing the following steps:

1. Select the source or originating cube (the cube you will be drilling from) and right-click on it (in TM1 Server Explorer).
2. Select **Create Drill Process...** from the menu.
3. At this point, a dialog opens displaying a list of parameter values for the origination (source) cube and all of the cube's dimensions.

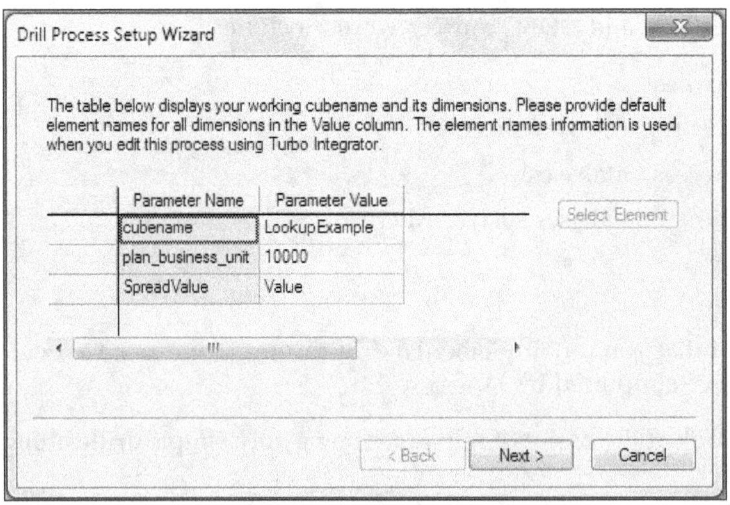

4. TM1 uses these values as parameters to the drill process when executing (drilling) from a source cube to a destination cube.
5. Click on **Next**, and the second dialog is displayed. Then, you can select the **Datasource Type** for your drill-to data.
6. At this point you need to define the data source that you selected in step 5.
7. For example, if you decide to use an ODBC data source, you will need to supply the following things:
    - **Datasource Name**: This is the official name given to the ODBC data source (DSN) that you want to access when drilling from your source cube. Remember that this DSN must be accessible to the machine where the TM1 Server is running.
    - **User Name**: This is the valid user name which TM1 will use to log into the ODBC data source that you are using.
    - **Password**: This is the password that the user name you set is to use.
    - **Query**: This is the query that defines the data or information to return from the ODBC data source. These results will be displayed in your drill-to window.
8. If you want to use an existing TM1 cube view as a data source, you need to supply the following:

    `TM1Servername:cubename:cubeviewname`

To select the **Datasource Type** as **Other**, you can click on the button labeled as **Launch TurboIntegrator**. This will open the **Data Source** tab in the TI window and allow you to create a custom TI process to define the dataset that you want to drill-to. This is by far the most powerful option to create a drill-through TI process because you can create dynamic views or modify existing views of detailed or otherwise relevant data to drill-through, based upon a variety of logic.

Once you have created the desired TI logic (you can refer to *Chapter 3, TurboIntegrator (TI)*), you can perform the following steps:

1. Click on **Finish**. The **Save Process As** dialog will open.
2. Enter a name for the drill process in the **Name** box.
3. Click on **Save**. Then, TM1 saves your drill process as a TI process, but prefixes the name with the string `}Drill_`.
4. For example, if you save a drill process with the name `SurfboardSalesCubeToODBCSource`, TM1 saves the process as `}Drill_SurfboardSalesCubeToODBCSource`.

> For best practice, we recommend that you use a drill process name that identifies the origination cube associated with the drill process. This type of naming convention makes it easier to identify a drill process name when you edit a drill process, or select from several drill processes associated with a cube—IBM

Drill process parameters

As mentioned earlier, when you create a drill process, Cognos TM1 sets up the parameters that are passed to the drill process. When you execute the drill process to drill from an origination cube to the detailed data, TM1 updates the parameter values to reflect the cube location from which the drill-through originates.

Unfortunately, you cannot add additional parameters to a drill process.

Editing drill processes

When you select a TM1 cube view as a data source in a drill-through, TM1 will automatically add some code to your TI drill-through process. The code which gets inserted is the TurboIntegrator function:

```
ReturnViewHandle('Cube','View')
```

This function gets inserted above or below the generated statements area, which is located on the **Epilog** sub-tab of the **Advanced** tab in the TurboIntegrator window.

> **Generated statements**
>
> You will recall from previous chapters of this book that a TI process includes four procedures that are executed one or more times in a sequence. Each of these sections (procedures) contains TM1 generated statements that are created for you automatically based on options you select elsewhere in the TI window.

Keep in mind that, if you change the data source for a drill process, earlier versions of TM1 will not go back and automatically update your drill-through process to change the `ReturnViewHandle` function with the new data source information because the function is outside the generated statements area.

You will have to edit the cube view data source in the `ReturnViewHandle` function for the drill process yourself. It is always a good idea to verify the `ReturnViewHandle` parameters after every change to a drill process, whether you change the data source or just make logic or coding changes to the TI process itself.

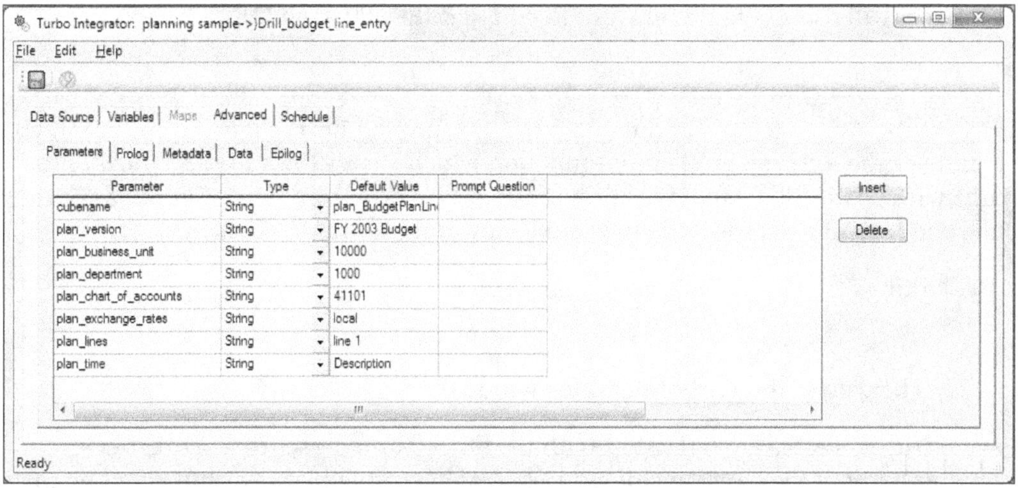

If you have created your drill-through by selecting **Datasource Type** as **ODBC**, TM1 does not require `ReturnViewHandle` to be inserted into the TI drill-through process (it uses `ReturnSQLTableHandle`—which does not require parameter changes like the `ReturnViewHandle` function does). When you use an ODBC data source, if you change your drill process to use a different ODBC data source, you do not have any function (`ReturnViewHandle`) to edit or change.

It is simple to edit an existing drill-through process from TM1 Server Explorer. From within Server Explorer, right-click on the source or origination cube (where you created the drill process or the cube that the drill process is associated with). From there, you can select (from the menu) **Drill** and then select **Edit Drill Process**. The **Select Drill Process** dialog will display all of the drill processes that are associated with this cube:

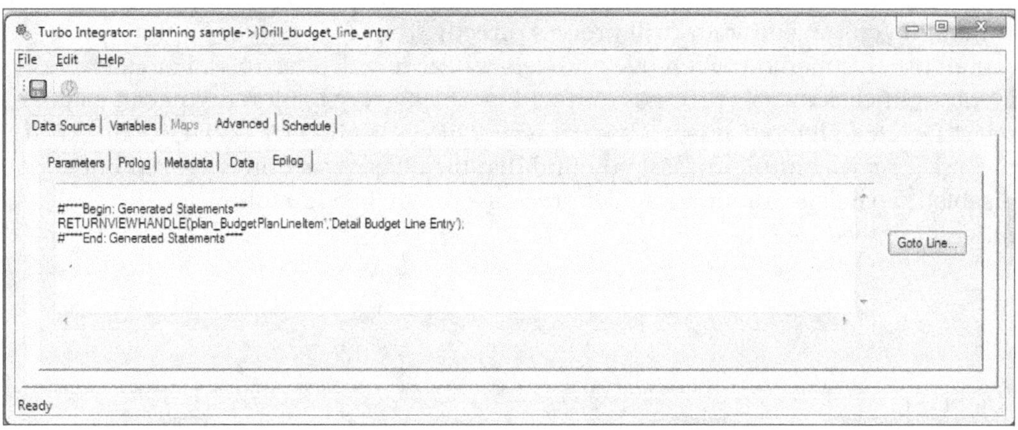

Select the drill process that you want to edit and then click on **OK**.

The TurboIntegrator window opens.

Click on the **Advanced** tab and then go to (click on) the **Epilog** tab. At this point, you should see the **ReturnViewHandle** function which shows the cube and view of the (cube view) data source that was previously set up. You can then edit or change the cube and/or view to reflect the new cube view data source to be used.

After editing:

1. Click on **Save**.
2. Then, close the TurboIntegrator window.

Saved drill processes are not listed with the other TI processes in TM1 Server Explorer because they are considered to be TM1 control objects (as indicated by the prefix of }). Of course, if you turn on the **Display Control Objects** option in Server Explorer, you will be able to see all of the current control objects, including all of the saved drill processes.

> **Viewing TM1 control objects**
> To make TM1 control objects visible in TM1 Server Explorer, you can click on the **View** menu item and then select **Display Control Objects**.

Once you have displayed the control objects within TM1 Server Explorer, you can then right-click on the drill process and select **Edit** to make changes. You can even right-click on your process and select **Run**, but it will not result in a cube view of your related data, it will only provide a message **Process completed successfully**.

Although you can edit your drill process directly from TM1 Server Explorer, you cannot use this method to remove or delete an existing drill process. For example, if you right-click on a TI process from within TM1 Server Explorer, you can usually select **Delete** to remove the process. However, if you right-click on an existing drill process (or any control process) you find that the deleted section is greyed out and disabled. To delete or remove a drill process you will need to follow a different procedure.

Removing drill processes

To remove an existing drill process, you need to perform the following steps:

1. From within TM1 Server Explorer, right-click on the source cube (the cube with which the drill process is associated).
2. Select **Drill**.
3. Then, select **Delete Drill Process**. The **Delete Drill Processes** dialog box opens which will list all of the drill processes associated with the cube.
4. Select the process(es) that you want to remove (delete).
5. Then, click on **OK**.

> To select multiple adjacent drill processes, you can click-and-drag across the processes. To select multiple non-adjacent processes, hold down *Ctrl*, and click on each drill process.

Drill rules

A drill assignment rule or drill rule is a rule that links cube cell areas with related or detailed data to be drilled-through to (the drill-to detailed or related data can reside in any existing TM1 cube on the same TM1 Server instance or reside in any ODBC accessible data, or really any data accessible through a TM1 TurboIntegrator process as discussed earlier).

Drill rules will launch (execute) the TI process that you specify for a specific cube cell area.

Feeders

Unlike other TM1 rules, drill-rules do not require the addition of any supporting feeders specifically to make the drill work.

Area definition

As a quick review from an earlier chapter of this book (*Chapter 4, Rules*), each rule must have an area definition to define for Cognos TM1 which cell values to calculate with a rule. Using areas you can specify which calculations apply to different parts of a cube.

For example, specific calculations may vary from region to region. So, you may need to apply different rules based upon the selected region.

The same area definition that you define for any TM1 rule can be used to define an area definition for a drill rule.

Creating a drill assignment rule

Although a drill rule is really just another TM1 rule, it is not visible when you open the TM1 Rules Editor in the usual way (discussed in an earlier chapter of this book). To create a TM1 drill rule you need to perform the following steps:

1. Right-click on the source cube (the cube you will be drilling from) from within TM1 Server Explorer.
2. Select **Drill**.
3. Then select **Create Drill Assignment Rule**. This will open the TM1 Rules Editor, but any non-drill rules that are currently associated with this cube will not be displayed:

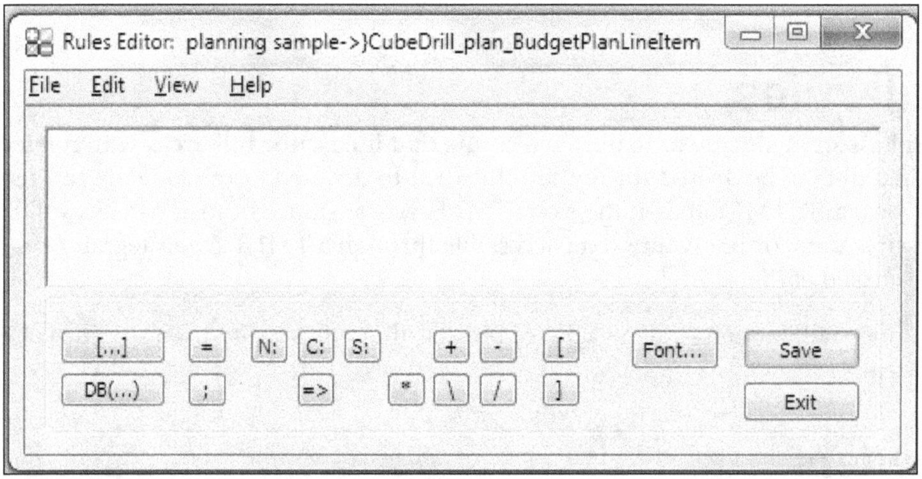

Once the Rules Editor is open, you can continue to create your drill rule.

First, as with any TM1 rule, you need to define the area within your cube that you want to associate with the drill-through.

The simplest area definition might be to associate all cells in the cube with the drill-through. To do this you can use the **Area** button in the Rules Editor, or simply type in the empty brackets `[]`.

To narrow the area definition (to reduce the number of cells in the cube that are associated with the drill-through), you should select the element or elements that define the cells you want to specifically associate with the detailed data.

Again, you can do this manually or use the Rules Editor by performing the following steps:

1. Click the **Area** button. When you do this the **Reference to Cube** dialog box opens.
2. Then, click on the **Dimension** button and select the elements that define the cells that you want to associate with the drill-through data.
3. Finally, click on **OK**:

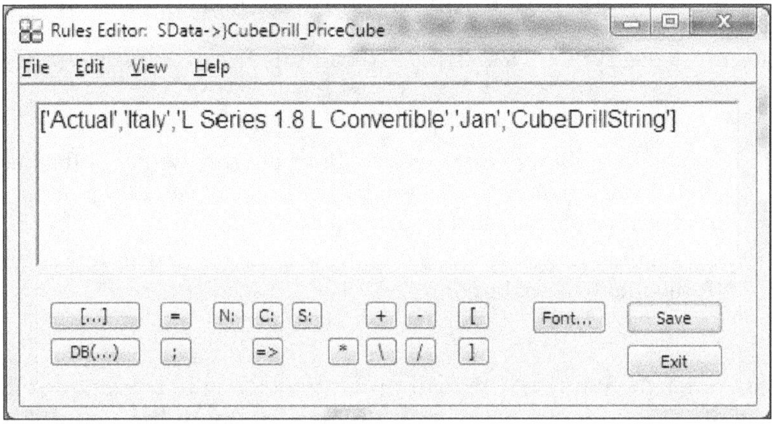

Drill-through area examples

Some examples of drill-through rule area definitions are as follows:

The following area definition would associate the drill process with all cells in the cube:

```
[]=
```

The following area definition would associate the drill process with only the dimension element named `Actual`:

```
['Actual']=
```

The following area definition would associate the drill process with only the dimension elements named `Actual` and `First Quarter`:

```
['Actual', 'First Quarter']=
```

The following area definition would implement the drill-through only for a version element with the string `Act` starting at position `6`:

```
# Filter out by Version
[] = S: IF(SUBST(!PPP_Version, 6, 3) @<> 'Act', '', CONTINUE);
```

Assigning drill processes

Once you have defined your drill rule area definition (described above), you can assign a drill process to the area. To do this type the equal sign and then `S:`.

All drill rules must use type `S:` for string—recall this from *Chapter 4, Rules*.

> Cognos TM1 allows you to create a link between two cubes that have related data. To do this, create a drill assignment rule. Keep in mind that this type of rule must be defined as a string.
>
> You should know that if you forget and define your drill rule as type `N:`, the rule will not be compiled.

Now, you can enter the name of the drill process enclosed in single quotation marks to define the detailed data which you want to associate with the area definition that you defined for your cube.

Remember that you should use proper naming conventions when you name your drill processes and do not add the prefix `}Drill` as TM1 will automatically add that prefix for you. For example, I might name my drill process as follows:

```
Launch_Sales_Transactions
```

Then, TM1 would rename it as follows:

```
}Drill_Launch_Sales_Transactions
```

An interesting fact!

You can associate more than one drill process with a drill process rule area definition by enclosing all of the drill process names, separated by commas, within a set of single quotation marks, as follows:

```
[]=s:'processname1,processname2';
```

If you do this, (as in the above example) when the user attempts to drill from the defined area, they will be presented with a simple **Select** dialog and they will have to select the drill process that they want to execute.

> It would be nice if all defined drill processes automatically executed upon a single drill operation, resulting in multiple detailed data views being opened at once, but this is not currently supported.

To terminate or end your drill rule you must add the semicolon at the end of your rule (as is the syntax for all TM1 rules and noted in *Chapter 4, Rules*).

> You must use a semicolon to end every rule statement.

The final step to create or define your drill rule is to click on **Save**.

You do this to compile your rule and associate it with the cube. If there are syntax errors, your rule will not compile and you will be presented with an error message.

More on drill rule area definitions

If your drill rule area definition is associated with a single source of detailed data, the data opens in a new (Cube Viewer) window.

If your drill rule area definition is associated with two or more sources of detailed data, a list of the data sources is displayed and you will have to select the source you want to view and click on **OK**.

When the relevant drill-to data resides in a cube, a new instance of the TM1 Cube Viewer opens, displaying the detailed data, but if the associated drill-to data resides in a relational database, Cognos TM1 displays the data in a Relational Drill-Through viewer. From there you can copy selected data to the clipboard.

Conditional drill rules

At some point you may want to add some additional logic to your drill process rule. You can use any valid TM1 Rules function to do this in your rule.

Some simple examples of this might be as follows:

```
# Sample drill number 1
#- Define the area - in this case the model dimension is used and the
#- area is defined as 'Standard #- Model'.  If the standard model in
the #- surfboard Meta cube is X then execute the drill process
#- named launch_standard_model
  ['Standard Model']=s:IF(DB('Surfboard Meta',!subclass, !version,
  'Standard Model')@='X','launch_Standard_Model','');
```

and

```
# Sample drill number 2
#- Define the area - in this case the model dimension is used and the
#- area is defined as 'Long
#- Board Model'.  If the long board model in the surfboard meta ube is
X #- then the user will be #- presented with a choice to execute the
drill #- process launch_long_board_model
```

or

```
#- launch_standard_model
  ['Long Board Model']=s:IF(DB('model_meta',!subclass,!version,'% of
  Channel')@='X','launch_long_board_model,launch_Standard_Model','');
```

Drilling from an Excel Slice

As specified in the TM1 Users Guide:

> *The Slice option, available from the Cube Viewer and In-Spreadsheet Browser, lets you save a cube view as a standard worksheet. When you create a slice, TM1 generates a worksheet populated with functions. These functions display the current database values in the worksheet.*

As we mentioned earlier in this chapter, it is possible to drill-through to related data from a Microsoft Excel worksheet (rather than the TM1 Cube Viewer).

We can follow these steps to slice the current cube view into a worksheet:

1. Open (or create a new) view in the Cognos TM1 Cube Viewer.
2. From the Cube Viewer, click on **File**.
3. Click on **Slice**. Then, TM1 slices the view into a new Excel worksheet.

At this point you should have your view sliced into a Microsoft Excel worksheet. Now, if you right-click on a cell in the worksheet (that corresponds to the area definition in your drill rule), TM1 will respond by drilling the data which is related to that cell into a new Excel worksheet within your current workbook.

Why does this work? Because the cells in the sliced worksheet contain the Cognos TM1 DBRW functions that retrieve and display the values from the Cognos TM1 cube. Therefore, the drill works!

Drilling from an Active Form

As specified in the TM1 Users Guide:

> *Active Forms let you view and update live TM1 cube data directly in Excel whenever you are connected to the TM1 server on which the cube data resides. Active Forms retain the ability to expand and collapse row dimension consolidations in a TM1 view while allowing you to use native Excel features and functions to create complex reports.*

Another place where drill-through works—other than the TM1 Cube Viewer and a sliced worksheet—is an Active Form. You can create your Active Form, using either of the following methods:

- From the TM1 Cube Viewer File menu, click on **Active Form Slice**.
- From the TM1 Cube Viewer toolbar, click on the **Active Form** button.

The Active Form is created in a new empty Excel worksheet and of course, right-clicking on your drill rule area definition will result in TM1 drilling the related data into a new worksheet within your workbook.

Drill-through performance

Drill-through is a great feature that Cognos TM1 supports. One of the most obvious uses for this functionality is to provide the ability to examine the transactional data that makes up a total. Although setting up a TM1 drill-through to capture and display underlying transactional data is straightforward, you as a developer should make every effort to optimize the performance of the drill. Areas to examine are SQL statement optimization, relational database indexing schemas, and even possibly restricting the maximum number of records that can be drilled to.

The following is a very simple example of restricting a drill-through by providing a minimum and maximum year range that is drillable. It checks the version selected in the drill-from cube for a year (all version names start with a `YYYY` year) and the year value in a system control cube (`Sys_TI_Variables`) and then does some math to determine if the year is within the predetermined range:

```
# Filter by date
# Filter out year less than min year - version names start with YYYY
[] = S:
  IF(SUBST(!PPP_Version, 1, 4) @< STR(NUMBR(SUBST(TODAY(1), 1, 4)) -
DB
  ( 'Sys_TI_Variables', 'Transaction_Details' , 'nVar4_Val' ), 4, 0)
  , '', CONTINUE);
# Filter in Year greater than min year
[] = S:
  IF(SUBST(!PPP_Version, 1, 4) @> STR(NUMBR(SUBST(TODAY(1), 1, 4)) -
DB
  ( 'Sys_TI_Variables', 'Transaction_Details' , 'nVar4_Val' ), 4,
  0),'KCSR_TD_ODBC', CONTINUE);
```

Summary

In this chapter, we have discussed the basics of the Cognos TM1 supported drill-through that you will need to know and be comfortable with before taking the current IBM Cognos TM1 Developer (Test COG-310) certification exam. We have also looked at some code examples.

In the next chapter, we will cover the definition, purpose, and use of virtual and lookup cubes in Cognos TM1.

Two minute drill

There are some important points which you must know about drill-through:

- The current certification exam assigns a weightage of 5 percent to the drill-through topic.
- To implement a TM1 drill-through, you can simply use one or more drill TurboIntegrator (TI) processes and one or more drill rules to associate a data intersection point (a cell) with detailed or related data.
- The components that make up the drill-through feature in Cognos TM1 are the drill process and the drill assignment rule.

- The drill processes that you create will define the detailed or related data that you want to assign to the drill-from data intersection point (the drill-from cell).
- The drill assignment rules that you create will define the relationship between the drill-from and the drill-to.
- Once you have created the drill-through TI processes and drill assignment rules, you can execute that process (by right-clicking on the drill-from cell) and open the detail (or associated) information in a new TM1 Cube Viewer window.
- There are basically three types of supported drill-through types—meaning that there are three ways to source your drill-to data.
- The three basic types of drill-through are cube views, ODBC, and other.
- You can define cube views that actually exceed the maximum amount of memory that Cognos TM1 can allocate when you access a view.
- `MaximunViewSize` is an optional `.cfg` file parameter. It sets the maximum size that a cube view can display.
- You can define a drill-through from an originating cube to any valid ODBC source as long as the ODBC source being drilled to is accessible from the computer on which the TM1 Server is running.
- Drill processes are simply TI processes that you create or define in a different way from the method of creating and saving TI processes described earlier in this book.
- The TM1 cube that is the source (displays the master or original data, or where the drill-through originates) is known as or is referred to as the origination cube.
- Steps to create the drill process are as follows:
    a. Select the source or origination cube and right-click.
    b. Then, from the menu select **Create Drill Process...**.
    c. At this point a dialog opens displaying a list of parameter values for the origination cube and all of the cube's dimensions.
    d. Click on **Next** and the second dialog will be displayed.
    e. Then, you can select **Datasource Type** for your drill-to data.
    f. Click on **Finish**. The **Save Process As** dialog will open.
    g. Enter a name for the drill process in the **Name** box.
    h. Click on **Save**. TM1 then saves your drill process as a TI process.

- For an ODBC drill-through, the data source name is the official name given to the ODBC data source (DSN) that you want to access when drilling from your source cube.
- TM1 saves your drill process with a `}Drill` prefix.
- When you select a TM1 cube view as **Datasource Type** in a drill-through, TM1 will automatically add some code to your TI drill-through process. The code which gets inserted is the TI function:

  ```
  ReturnViewHandle('Cube','View')
  ```

- If you have created your drill-through using a **Datasource Type** of ODBC, TM1 does not require the `ReturnViewHandle` function to be inserted into the TI drill-through process (it uses `ReturnSQLTableHandle`—which does not require parameter changes like the `ReturnViewHandle` function does).
- Saved drill processes are not listed with the other TI processes in TM1 Server Explorer because they are considered to be TM1 control objects (as indicated by the prefix of }). Of course, if you turn on the **Display Control Objects** option in Server Explorer, you will then be able to see all of the current control objects, including all of the saved drill processes.
- To make the TM1 control objects visible in TM1 Server Explorer, you can click on the **View** menu item and then select **Display Control Objects**.
- Once you have displayed the control objects within TM1 Server Explorer, you can then right-click on the drill process and select **Edit** to make changes to your drill process.
- A drill assignment rule or drill rule is a rule that links cube cell areas with related or detailed data to be drilled-through to. The drill-to detailed or related data can reside in any existing TM1 cube on the same TM1 Server instance or reside in any ODBC accessible data, or really any data accessible through a TM1 TurboIntegrator process as discussed earlier.
- The same area definition that you define for any TM1 rule can be used to define an area definition for a drill rule.
- All drill rules must use type `S:` for string—recall this from *Chapter 4, Rules*.
- You can associate more than one drill process with a drill process rule area definition by enclosing all of the drill process names, separated by commas, within a set of single quotation marks.
- If your drill rule area definition is associated with two or more sources of detailed data, a list of the data sources gets displayed and you will have to select the source you want to view and click on **OK**.

- When the relevant drill-to data resides in a cube, a new instance of the TM1 Cube Viewer opens, displaying the detailed data, but if the associated drill-to data resides in a relational database, Cognos TM1 displays the data in a Relational Drill-Through viewer. From there you can copy selected data to the clipboard.
- It is possible to drill-through to related data from a Microsoft Excel worksheet (rather than the TM1 Cube Viewer).

Self-test

- **Question**: What is drill-through?

  Response: Drill-through can be described as the act of exploring related information.

- **Question**: What is one of the native powers of TM1?

  Response: Its native power is its ability to quickly consolidate values defined within a dimension.

- **Question**: What are the major components of drill-through?

  Response: The components that make up the drill-through feature in Cognos TM1 are the drill process and the drill assignment rule.

- **Question**: How do you define or relate data between the drill-from and drill-to?

  Response: The drill processes that you create will define the detailed or related data that you want to assign to the drill-from data intersection point (the drill-from cell).

- **Question**: What is the most common drill-through source?

  Response: Typically you set up a drill-through with the intention of drilling from a cell in a view in an open Cube Viewer. Keep in mind that you can also drill from a view that is displayed in an Excel Slice as well as from an Active Form.

- **Question**: What are the three drill-through types?

  Response: There are basically three types of supported drill-through types—meaning that there are three ways to source your drill-to data. They are cube views, ODBC, and other.

- **Question**: What is a cube view drill-through?

  Response: This type of drill-through is drilling from an originating TM1 cube view to any other cube view of data. You can literally drill-through to any saved or dynamically defined cube view as long as it resides on the same TM1 Server as the origination cube view.

- **Question**: What is the `MaximumViewSize` parameter used for?

  Response: This is an optional parameter. It sets the maximum size that a cube view can display. This can be any cube view—not just a drilled-to cube view.

- **Question**: What is the format of the `MaximumViewSize` parameter?

  Response: The format is `MaximumViewSize=n`, where n represents the amount of memory in MB to be allocated.

- **Question**: Give some examples of a drill-trough type of ODBC.

  Response: Some examples of valid ODBC sources would include dBase files, Microsoft Excel worksheets, MS Access databases, and relational databases such as Microsoft SQL Server.

- **Question**: What does the drill-through type of other mean?

  Response: The drill-through type in which you can implement a drill-through from any TM1 cube view to any data source supported by TI.

- **Question**: What is a drill process?

  Response: Drill processes are simply TI processes that you create or define in a different way from the method of creating and saving non drill-through TI processes. A drill-through process is used to define the detailed or related data (the data that will ultimately be displayed or opened in a new window). The TM1 cube that is the source (displays the master or original data, or where the drill-through originates) is known as or is referred to as the origination cube.

- **Question**: What is another way to describe a drill process?

  Response: Another way to think about a drill process is that it is the Cognos TM1 object that is used to specify the connection information in a drill-through.

- **Question**: Give the steps to create a drill process.

  Response: The steps are as follows:

  a. Select the source or origination cube and right-click on it (in TM1 Server Explorer).
  b. From the menu, select **Create Drill Process...**.
  c. At this point a dialog opens displaying a list of parameter values for the origination (source) cube and all of the cube's dimensions.
  d. Click on **Next**, and the second dialog is displayed.
  e. Then, you can select **Datasource Type** for your drill-to data.
  f. Once you have created the desired TurboIntegrator logic (you can refer to *Chapter 3, Turbointegrator (TI)*), you can click on **Finish**.
  g. The **Save Process As** dialog will open.
  h. Enter a name for the drill process in the **Name** box. Click on **Save**.

- **Question**: What happens when TM1 saves your drill process?

  Response: TM1 saves your drill process as a TI process, but prefixes the name with the string `}Drill`.

- **Question**: Can you change or add parameters to a drill process?

  Response: Unfortunately, you cannot add parameters to a drill process.

- **Question**: When you select a TM1 cube view as **Datasource Type** in a drill-through, TM1 will automatically add some code to your TI drill-through process. What is the code which gets inserted?

  Response: `ReturnViewHandle('Cube','View')`, this function gets inserted above or below the generated statements area.

- **Question**: If you have created your drill-through using a **Datasource Type** of ODBC, TM1 does not require the `ReturnViewHandle` function to be inserted into the TI drill-through process. What function does it insert?

  Response: It uses `ReturnSQLTableHandle`—which does not require parameter changes like the `ReturnViewHandle` function does.

- **Question**: How do you view TM1 control objects?

  Response: To make the TM1 control objects visible in TM1 Server Explorer, you can click on the **View** menu item and then select **Display Control Objects**.

- **Question**: Can you delete or remove a drill process directly from Server Explorer?

  Response: Although you can edit your drill process directly from TM1 Server Explorer, you cannot use this method to remove or delete an existing drill process.

- **Question**: How do you delete or remove a drill process?

  Response: To remove an existing drill process, you need to right-click the source cube and then select **Drill | Delete Drill Process**. The **Delete Drill Processes** dialog box opens which will list all of the drill processes associated with the cube. Select the process(es) that you want to remove (delete) and then click on **OK**.

- **Question**: What is a drill rule?

  Response: A drill assignment rule or drill rule is a rule that links cube cell areas with related or detailed data to be drilled-through to.

- **Question**: What is the purpose of a drill rule?

  Response: Drill rules launch (execute) the TI process that you specify for a specific cube cell area.

- **Question**: How do you create a drill assignment rule?

  Response: Right-click on the source cube and then select **Drill**. Then select **Create Drill Assignment Rule**. This will open TM1 Rules Editor. Once the Rules Editor is open, you can continue to create your drill rule. First, as with any TM1 rule, you need to define the area within your cube that you want to associate with the drill-through.

- **Question**: What type do all drill assignment rules need to be?

  Response: All drill rules must use type `S:` for string.

- **Question**: Are all drill assignment rules limited to a single drill process?

  Response: You can associate more than one drill process with a drill process rule area definition by enclosing all of the drill process names, separated by commas, within a set of single quotation marks.

- **Question**: How do you end or terminate a drill assignment rule?

  Response: To terminate or end your drill rule you must add a semicolon at the end of your rule.

- **Question**: Name some ways to ensure proper drill-through performance.

  Response: Areas to examine are SQL statement optimization, relational database indexing schemas, and even possibly restricting the maximum number of records that can be drilled-to.

7

Virtual and Lookup Cubes

In this chapter, we will learn the definition and purpose of both virtual and lookup cubes in Cognos TM1 with regards to the current IBM Cognos TM1 Developer (Test COG-310) certification exam.

The current certification exam assigns a weightage of 10 percent to this topic.

TM1 cube types

There are four types of cubes in Cognos TM1. They are as follows:

- Standard cubes
- Control cubes
- Virtual cubes
- Lookup cubes

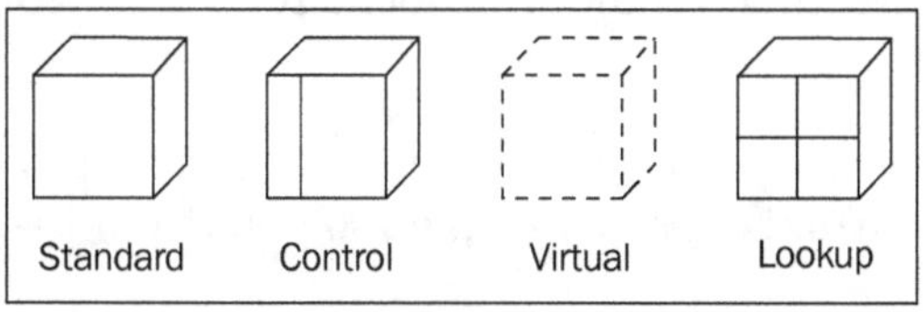

- **Virtual**: This term has been defined in philosophy as that which is not real but may display the salient qualities of the real—Wikipedia.
- **Lookup**: This term usually refers to searching a data structure for an item that satisfies some specified property—Wikipedia.

A standard cube in Cognos TM1 is referred to as a hard cube or a cube where data is actually loaded and resides.

In *Chapter 2, Dimensions and Cubes* we talked about the standard Cognos TM1 cube as well as dimension objects. You will remember following points:

- Cubes are to TM1 what tables are to relational databases.
- You can create a cube with dimensions, and dimensions identify how to organize the information or data that you want to track and report on.
- Each element in each dimension identifies the location (or "x-y coordinate") of a cell in a cube.
- Data is loaded into these cube cells and these cells are identified by the intersection of dimensions.

Virtual cubes

A virtual cube differs from a standard cube in Cognos TM1. It is a TM1 cube which is sometimes termed as a soft cube where no data is loaded to or resides in, but only references data points in other cubes.

Being a fully rules-calculated cube, virtual cubes have no data stored in them. They just have rules pulling data from other cubes and possibly performing additional calculations on that data.

To a TM1 user, a virtual cube may have the exact same appearance of a standard or hard cube. We will discuss the creation and use of a virtual cube in this chapter.

Virtual cube creation

To create a virtual cube, you would first design and create a cube using the methods already discussed for creating a standard cube, but no data would actually be loaded into the cube.

Standard TM1 cubes may have significant amounts of data pulled from or referenced from other cubes, but virtual cubes will have 100 percent of their data pulled from other cubes.

The steps to create a simple virtual cube are as follows:

1. From TM1 Server Explorer, right-click on **Cubes** and then select **Create New Cube**. The **Creating Cube** dialog will be opened. The **Available Dimensions** list (on the left) will list the current dimensions stored on the server.
2. Type a name for your virtual cube in the **Cube Name** field.

3. In the **Available Dimensions** box, select the dimensions that you want to include in your virtual cube.
4. Click on **Create Cube** to create your virtual cube.
5. Select your virtual cube from the cubes list.

Your virtual cube is now created! As with other Cognos TM1 cubes, to pull data from a source cube into your virtual cube, you will utilize TM1 rules.

To write the appropriate TM1 cube rules to associate with your virtual cube that will pull data from other cubes in TM1 into your virtual cube, you will have to perform the following steps:

1. If you right-click on your virtual cube name in TM1 Server Explorer, you can select **Create Rule**. Then, the TM1 Rules Editor will be displayed.
2. Create rules that reference or pull data points from other TM1 cubes.

Virtual cube rule association

As with all TM1 cubes, the rules that pull data from a source cube into a virtual cube must be associated with that virtual cube. Cognos TM1 displays an icon for each cube (including virtual cubes) that has rules associated with it:

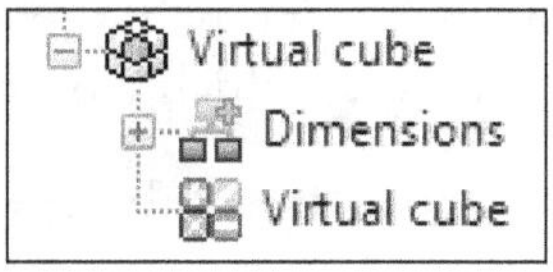

Feeders

Recalling our discussion on rules in *Chapter 2, Dimensions and Cubes*, it is important to remember that the more rules you implement, the more overall cube performance will be impacted. Specifically, the native consolidation ability of Cognos TM1 will slow down. To address this performance issue, you must make use of the `SKIPCHECK` and various individual `FEEDERS` declarations.

Adding rules to a cube will impact TM1's ability to utilize its sparse consolidation algorithm. Fortunately, you can tell TM1 where to look for rules-derived values with feeders that you create.

Intercube feeders

When working with intercube rules, as in the case of virtual cubes, rule statements reside in the target (the virtual) cube, while feeder statements always reside in the source cube.

It may be easier to understand if you think of your feeders pushing and pulling. Feeders do the pushing of data from the source cube (so, they will reside in or be associated with the source cube) while rules do the pulling of data into the destination cube (so, they will reside in or be associated with the destination cube). This is true for standard TM1 cubes as well as virtual TM1 cubes.

For example, if the virtual cube references data in the standard cube, the TM1 rules to reference the data in the standard cube will be associated with the virtual cube. The feeders to support these rules will reside in the standard cube:

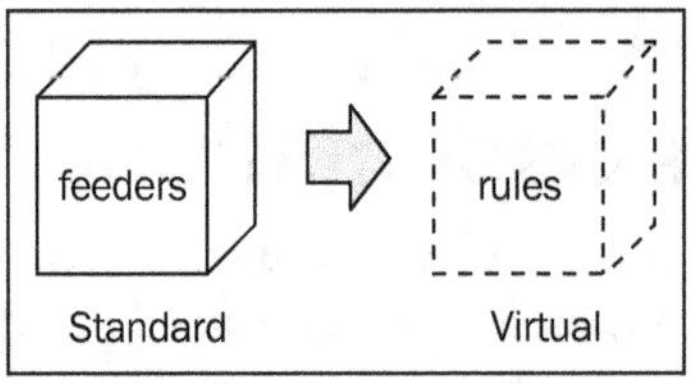

To create rules for a TM1 virtual cube, referencing reference data in other cubes, you have to understand rule cube references, which we explained in *Chapter 4, Rules*.

Now, let us look at some very simple virtual cube examples.

Submitting a forecast to a virtual cube

Suppose you had a global TM1 application with multiple cubes defined—possibly a cube for each of a company's sales regions—Northern, Western, Southern, and Eastern.

Each sales region cube holds forecasting data for only that particular region. At some point in the forecasting cycle, the regions need to submit a finished forecast for their region to corporate headquarters into a Global TM1 cube as part of a consolidated forecast for the organization.

Let us say that each of the global region cubes are made up of the following dimensions:

- Version
- Period
- Region
- Product
- Measure

You could create another hard cube and write a **TurboIntegrator** (**TI**) process to copy forecasts from each of the region cubes to the main cube to show your consolidated forecast.

Another solution might be to define the additional cube to consolidate all of the regions' forecasts for reporting, but instead of periodically copying data from the individual hard cubes to the consolidation cube, this cube could be a virtual cube using TM1 rules to reference or pull data from each of the source cubes:

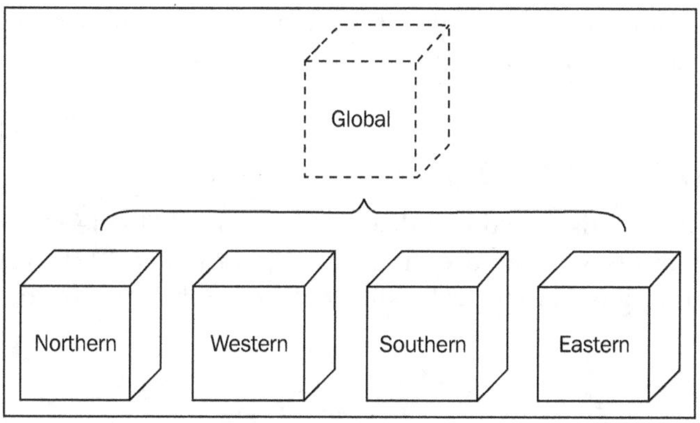

To do this you would create a rule in the virtual cube:

```
['Current Forecast','Northern']=N:DB('Northern','Actual',!Period,!Regi
on,!Product,'Current Forecast');
```

The above rule specifies an area definition for all cells that are associated with the version named `Current Forecast` and the region named `Northern`.

For these cells, the `DB` function would pull the value for the measure `Current Forecast` from the (source) cube named `Northern` for the currently selected period, region, and product. You could create a rule to pull `Current Forecast` from each of the source cubes into the consolidation cube.

The other cube reference rules are as follows:

```
['Current Forecast','Western']=N:DB('Western','Actual',!Period,!Region
,!Product,'Current Forecast');
 ['Current Forecast','Eastern']=N:DB('Eastern','Actual',!Period,!Regio
n,!Product,'Current Forecast');
 ['Current Forecast','Southern']=N:DB('Southern','Actual',!Period,!Reg
ion,!Product,'Current Forecast');
```

Using this method, forecast information entered into any of the hard cubes would be available immediately in the consolidation or virtual cube. No intervention would be required—such as running a TI process—to copy the data and make it available!

Unmatched dimensionality

In the above example, the global (or consolidated) cube is made up of identical dimensionality, that is, each of the region cubes making the TM1 rule easy and straightforward. In practice, these cubes may not have matched dimensionality and you will need to add logic to your rules to resolve these differences. Additionally, even when cube dimensionality matches, specific elements may require translation between source and destination cubes.

Conditional rules

In *Chapter 4, Rules*, we discussed the idea that Cognos TM1 rules can be written with conditional evaluation (you can use the `IF` function to force TM1 to evaluate a rule differently depending on a logic test). This feature can be utilized in our virtual cube example.

Using conditional rules within a virtual cube

Sometimes, it might be more realistic to wait until data is in a complete or approved state before making that data available in the consolidation cube, yet it is not desirable to have to intervene for sending or copying the data. One way to accomplish this might be to use conditional logic to modify your rule slightly:

```
 ['Current Forecast','Northern']=N:IF(DB('SysCntrl', 'Northern', 'Fore
castStatus')=1,DB('Northern','Actual',!Period,!Region,!Product,'Curre
nt Forecast'),0);
```

In the above rule, you can see that an application cube named `SysCntrl` is used to hold a flag named `ForecastStatus`. If this flag is set to a value of `1`, the forecast information for the region `Northern` is made available in the consolidation cube. Otherwise the forecast shows as a zero value in the consolidation cube.

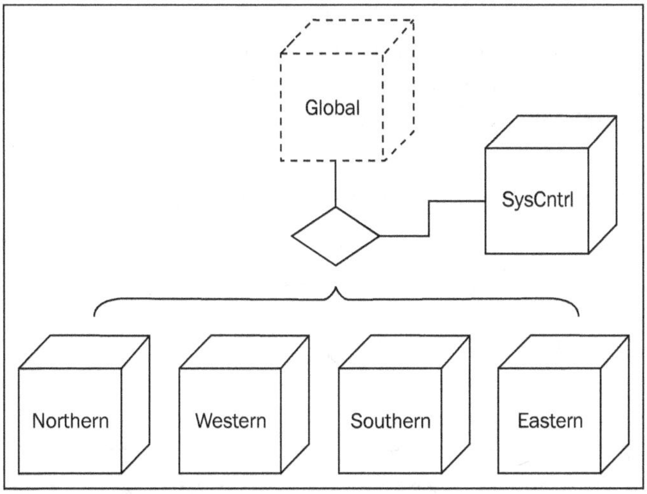

In practice, when a new forecast version is created, our system control cube (`SysCntrl`) value for `ForecastStatus` would be set to a value of `0` and some method would be provided to the region forecasters to set that value (for their respective region) to a `1` when their forecast is completed and ready to be submitted to the headquarters cube (of course, this is a very simple example and there is more to this—in practice you will have to deal with multiple versions, rule calculated versus static values, and so on.).

When using conditional logic in your rules you should always consider the effect on your approach to cube feeding. Just as your rules can utilize conditional logic, so can your feeders.

Consolidating data with a virtual cube

Another example of using a virtual cube is entity consolidation. For example, suppose a corporation consists of several legal entities that must report their financials to the parent. The parent as well as each **legal entity** (**LE**) has its own **Profit and Loss** (**P&L**) cube in TM1. The parent's financial reports must include all of the legal entities. To do this we could make the parent's P&L cube a virtual cube that includes rules that pull from each of the entities in the P&L cubes.

So, for example, in the parent P&L cube we have:

```
['8151', 'Legal Entity 1'] =N: DB('LegalEntity1 P&L','8151',!Legal_
Entity,!Version,!_Source,!_Period,!_Currency);
```

The above rule will pull the value for the account `8151` for the entity `Legal Entity 1` into the parent cube. Of course, it might be wise to not specify the account `8151` so that all accounts that exist in both the parent and entity cube will be pulled in without having to have a rule for each of the accounts:

```
['Legal Entity 1'] =N: DB('LegalEntity1 P&L',!Account',!Legal_
Entity,!Version,!_Source,!_Period,!_Currency);
```

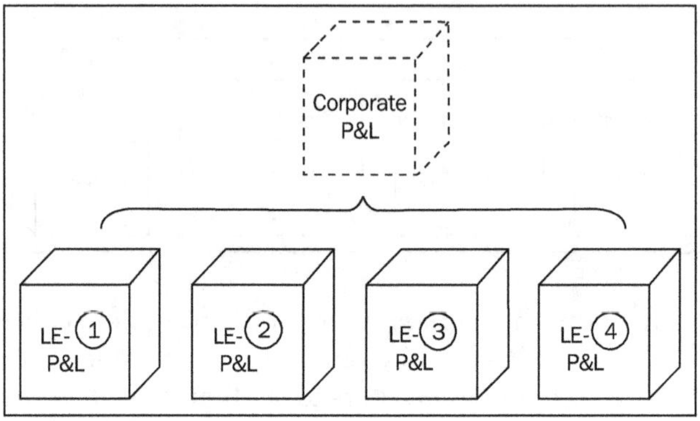

The parent cube most likely will have other rules that will calculate specific P&L values such as earnings per share, gross profit, and so on.

Reporting with virtual cubes

Another area where you can benefit from virtual cubes is with reporting. Some Cognos TM1 cubes may be very complicated, large, or have intensive rule calculations. In other examples, data required for a report may be sourced from multiple cubes. In these cases, specific end user reporting may become difficult (especially for the more casual TM1 user) or somewhat slow. Defining several specific reporting virtual cubes—based upon unique views of the larger cube or cubes—can be a solution:

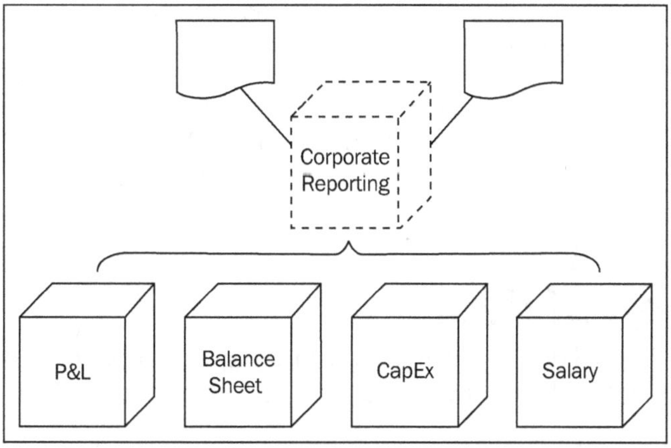

Other advantages of virtual cubes

The use of virtual cubes in your solution may also simplify the development of some TM1 active reports and websheets by centralizing information into a single location. In fact, some active reports may not be possible without the use of a virtual cube.

For other software, your organization may use TM1 cubes as a reporting source and may require all data to be located in a single cube. Of course, the performance must be evaluated and may require that you use a standard TM1 cube loaded with static data in some cases.

Additional reporting options

Before choosing to implement virtual cubes as part of your reporting solution, all of the other options provided by Cognos TM1 should be explored and considered. These options are discussed in *Chapter 9, Data Presentation and Reporting*.

Lookup cubes

Finally, another type of TM1 cube is the cube referred to as a lookup or conversion cube. This is a sort of utility cube. Lookup cubes are cubes that you can set up and use to support other cubes and processes within a TM1 application.

These cubes are most often set up to be read-only by design or even made non-visible to TM1 users and may contain calculations, controls, or reference data that are then used in your TM1 processing or pulled into other cubes using TM1 rules.

Keep in mind that before you create a lookup cube, you should review the existing TM1 control cubes to see if the data that is needed is available there.

As in any application there may be a need to share the same data or logic in multiple components of a Cognos TM1 application. Lookup cubes can be used here to eliminate redundancy of reference data used within TM1 cubes and processes on the same TM1 Server.

Translation of data

Whenever there is a need to perform a translation or conversion of information, you have to decide whether it is best to use an element attribute or a lookup cube.

Typically, if it is a single point translation (which involves only one dimension), you would have to use an attribute. If the translation involves multiple points, then you would use a lookup cube.

For example, one of the most common single point translations might be the translation of an account code from a system external to your Cognos TM1 system to an accounting code in a company's general ledger system or a code more commonly used by your TM1 system users.

Rather than writing custom program code that might need to be changed later if an account code changes in one of the systems or for other reasons, a much better option would be to implement a two dimensional lookup cube for this translation.

This lookup cube would have the source system account code dimension as its first dimension and a measures dimension that would include the element `GL Account` as its second dimension.

Then, you could write the following lines of code in a TI process to convert or transform the code as you are loading it:

```
AcctLkUpCubeName = 'AcctLkUp';
GLAcct = CellGetS(AcctLkUpCubeName, AccountID, GLAccountMeasure);
```

In the above example code, `AccountID` is the source system account ID and the variable `GLAcct` will hold the account code in the corporate general ledger system. The value in `GLAccountMeasure` can be a parameter passed to the TI process to make the process even more flexible.

> One advantage of using a lookup cube of this kind is that additional measures can be added in the future, which you would need to translate the source system account code to additional values, and no changes to the TI process would be required.

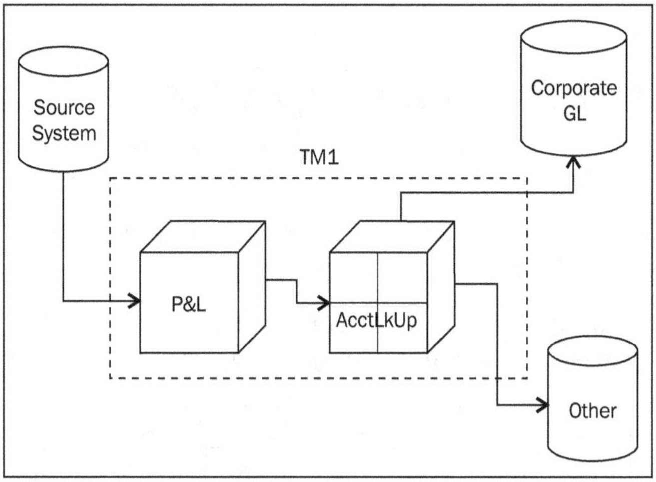

Lookup cubes are not usually intended for direct use by the end user. So, it is a good idea to name your lookup cubes with the Cognos TM1 control cube prefix `}`.

In the above example, you might name the lookup cube as `}AcctLkUp`.

By default, Cognos TM1 does not display cubes with this prefix in TM1 Server Explorer but, if required, a user can make these cubes visible. The specific behavior of Cognos TM1 control cubes was covered in *Chapter 2, Dimensions and Cubes*.

You may choose to utilize the TM1 control cube prefix or may not, when naming your lookup cubes, but using a consistent naming convention will make it easy to quickly identify and reference all lookup cubes in the TM1 instance.

Lookup cube example—using rules

All rules that utilize lookup cubes depend on the TM1 Rules `DB` function.

Here is another lookup example:

Surfboards are sold in different lengths. The price of each board will be based upon a different price per foot. A `Cost` cube holds information on the cost of surfboards; a lookup cube holds the price per foot reference data.

A rule will be written to yield the total cost of each surfboard sold.

The rule in the `Cost` cube might be as follows:

```
['Board Cost'] = ['Board Length']* DB('Cost',!Product,'PricePerFoot');
```

In this example, you can see that the reference cube might be the single source for pricing information in the TM1 application.

Loading data with lookup cubes

For performance reasons, lookup cubes can also be used to load data into a TM1 application without locking the cubes that your users see and use.

In a scenario like this, you can define one or more lookup cubes to which TI processes would load the data.

Another cube (or cubes) will then use TM1 rules to reference the data in the lookup cube and would then be used by users for reporting or other updating.

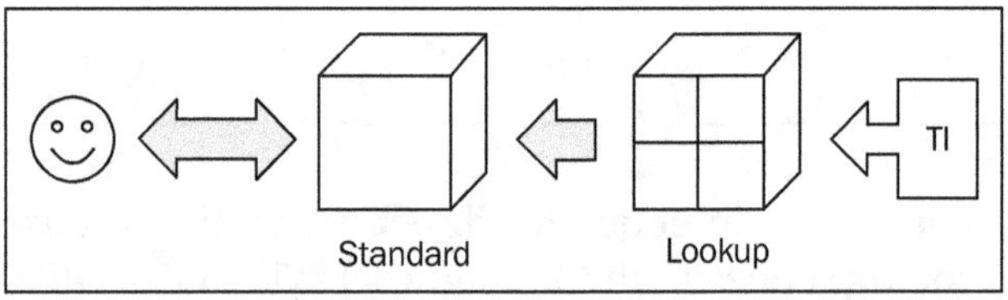

Finally, a reporting cube may be defined at a certain level of aggregation. This means that only data at an aggregated level is loaded in an available cube while a lookup cube (or cubes) is utilized to hold transactional detail level data which can be viewed by the user through the use of the TM1 drill-through feature (which we described in *Chapter 6, Drill-through*).

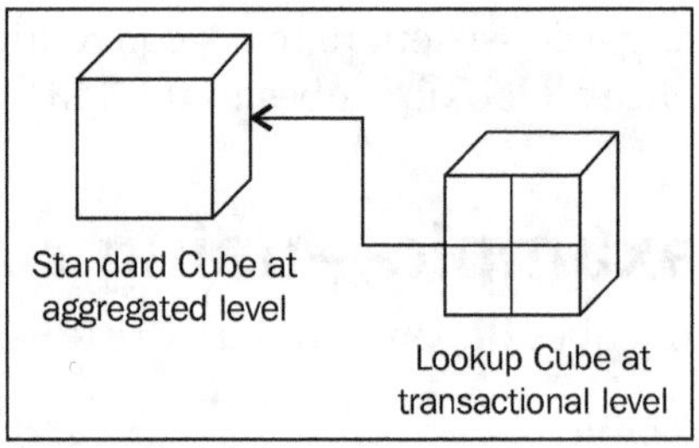

This is a simple (but practical) example of giving users the ability to view and report on sales total aggregations while also having specific transactional data available to them if required for supporting specifically selected totals.

Spreading data with lookup cubes

Cognos TM1 provides numerous types of pre-defined data spreading functions. These functions are useful for quickly distributing data to selected cells in a Cognos TM1 cube.

From the TM1 Cube Viewer, In-Spreadsheet Browser, and in slice worksheets you can right-click on a cell and TM1 will offer a menu that includes **Data Spread** where you can then click to select the desired data spreading method.

This is another opportunity to use a TM1 lookup cube—to support the data spreading method called Relative Proportional Spread.

The Relative Proportional Spread method spreads values to the children of a consolidation—proportional to the children of a reference cell. That reference cell can be located in a lookup cube in the same TM1 instance.

You could create a lookup cube using the key dimension in your standard spread-to cube so that it uses the same hierarchy as that cube does. The other lookup cube dimension would hold the spreading values.

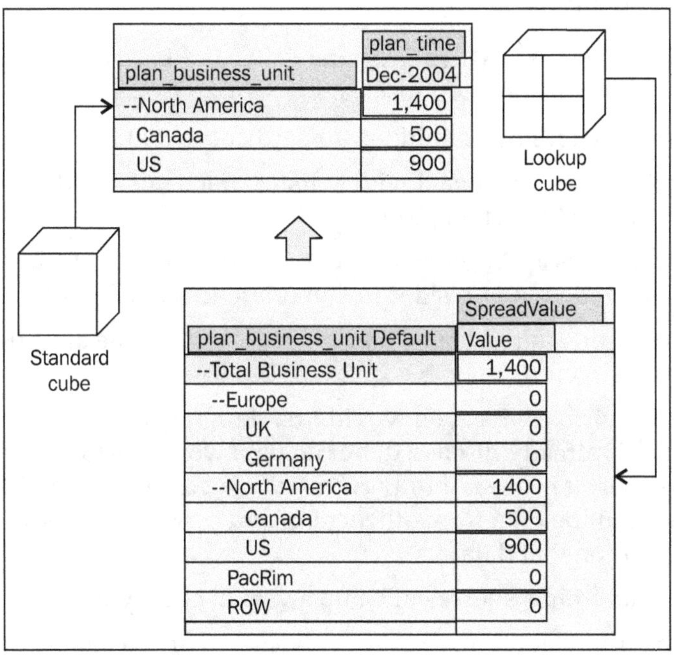

Summary

In this chapter, we have discussed the basics of Cognos TM1 virtual and lookup cubes focusing on what you will need to know and be comfortable with before taking the current IBM Cognos TM1 Developer (Test COG-310) certification exam. We have also looked at some practical examples.

In *Chapter 8, Time Considerations*, we will discuss the importance and use of the time dimension in Cognos TM1.

Two minute drill

There are some important points about virtual and lookup cubes:

- There are four types of cubes in Cognos TM1. They are as follows:
    - Standard cubes
    - Control cubes
    - Virtual cubes
    - Lookup cubes
- A standard Cognos TM1 cube is referred to as a hard cube or a cube where data is actually loaded and resides.
- TM1 control cubes by definition, are hard cubes that hold data.
- All control cubes are named with a first character of } and are by default not-visible within TM1 Server Explorer.
- A virtual cube is a TM1 cube which is referred to as a soft cube where no data actually is loaded to or resides in, but references data points in other cubes.
- To a TM1 user, a virtual cube may have the exact same appearance as a standard hard cube.
- To create a virtual cube, you would first design and create a cube using the methods already discussed, but no data would be loaded into the cube because a virtual cube is a fully rules-calculated cube. There is no data stored, just rules pulling data from other cubes and possibly performing additional calculations on that data.
- To pull data from a source cube into a virtual cube, you utilize TM1 rules.
- Rules that pull data from a source cube into a virtual cube must be associated with the virtual cube.

- You can define a virtual cube to consolidate all of the regions forecasts for reporting using TM1 rules to reference or pull data from each of the source cubes.
- Another example of using a virtual cube is entity consolidation.
- Another way to take advantage of virtual cubes is by reporting.
- Defining several specific virtual cubes—based upon unique views of the larger cube or cubes—can improve performance for user reporting.
- Lookup cubes are cubes that you can set up and use to support other cubes within a TM1 application.
- Lookup cubes are usually read-only or even made non-visible to the user and may contain calculations or reference data that are then pulled into other cubes using TM1 rules.
- Whenever there is a need to perform a translation or conversion of information, you have to decide whether to use an element attribute or a lookup cube.
- In a single point translation (involves only one dimension), you would use an attribute.
- For multiple point translations, you would use lookup cube.
- One of the most common single point translations would be translating an account code from a source system to an accounting code in a company's general ledger system.
- One advantage of using a lookup cube is additional measures which could be added in the future that you would need to translate the source system account code to additional values and no changes to the TI process would be required.
- Lookup cubes are not usually for end users. So, it is a good idea to name your lookup cubes with the Cognos TM1 control cube prefix }.
- Lookup cubes can also be used to load data into a TM1 application without locking the cubes which the users see and use.

Self test

- **Question**: What are the four basic types of cubes in Cognos TM1?

  Response: Standard cubes, control cubes, virtual cubes, and lookup cubes.

- **Question**: What is a hard cube?

  Response: A standard cube in Cognos TM1 is referred to as a hard cube. It is a cube where data is actually loaded and resides.

- **Question**: Where does Cognos TM1 store data?

  Response: Cubes are to TM1 what tables are to relational databases. Almost all data stored in TM1 is stored in and accessed from cubes.

- **Question**: What are the ways to create standard TM1 cubes?

  Response: There are two ways to create (standard) cubes:

  - **Empty cube**: You can create an empty cube by selecting (at least) two dimensions from the list of existing dimensions in the **Creating Cube** window to create a new cube with no data.
  - **External data sources**: You can create a cube and load it with data by using TI to identify and map dimensions and data from an external data source to a new or existing cube (of course, this requires some expertise using TurboIntegrator).

- **Question**: How many dimensions must a TM1 cube have?

  Response: Each and every TM1 cube must have at least two dimensions and a maximum of 256 dimensions.

- **Question**: Where does data get loaded into a TM1 cube?

  Response: Data is loaded into cube cells. A cell is identified by the intersection of dimensions.

- **Question**: What is the maximum size allowed for dimensions?

  Response: Dimension names can have a maximum of 256 characters.

- **Question**: How can data be loaded into a TM1 cube?

  Response: Data can be loaded using Excel worksheets or manually through the Cube Viewer.

- **Question**: What is a quick way to distribute data across cells in a cube?

  Response: TM1 provides a feature called spreading. Using spreading, an application developer can quickly populate a large number of cells in a cube with the same data.

- **Question**: What is the most flexible way of loading data into a TM1 cube?

  Response: The most flexible and effective method to load a cube with data is through the use of a custom TI process.

- **Question**: What is the first step that usually needs to be performed before loading data into a TM1 cube?

  Response: Before data can be loaded, the data's destination within the cube should be first cleared or zeroed out.

- **Question**: What if there are more fields in a data source than there are in a TM1 cube?

  Response: Depending upon the detail level of the data to be loaded and the structure of the cube that the data is to be loaded into, you may need to accumulate or consolidate the data up to the level supported by the cube to load it.

- **Question**: What is the definition of a TM1 control cube?

  Response: Special cubes created and used by TM1 are referred to as control cubes (also, by definition, these control cubes are hard cubes that hold data).

- **Question**: What does TM1 use the control cubes for?

  Response: The cubes that TM1 uses to perform certain activities are called control cubes. These activities are security, client and group administration, object attribute and properties control, performance monitoring, and hold tracking by username.

- **Question**: How can you identify a TM1 control cube?

  Response: All control cubes are named with a first character of } and are by default non-visible within TM1 Server Explorer. These cubes can be made visible by selecting **View** and then selecting **Display Control Objects**.

- **Question**: What is a TM1 virtual cube?

  Response: A virtual cube is a TM1 cube which is referred to as a soft cube where no data is loaded to or resides in but references data points in other cubes.

- **Question**: How will a virtual cube appear to a user?

  Response: To a TM1 user, a virtual cube may have the exact same appearance as a standard or hard cube.

- **Question**: How do you create a virtual cube?

  Response: To create a virtual cube, first you would have to design and create a cube using the methods already discussed to create a standard cube, but no data would be loaded into the cube because a virtual cube is a fully rules-calculated cube.

- **Question**: How do you load data into a virtual cube?

  Response: There is no data stored, just rules pulling data from other cubes and possibly performing additional calculations on that data.

- **Question**: How do you pull data into a virtual cube?

  Response: To pull data from a source cube into a virtual cube, you can utilize TM1 rules.

- **Question**: What do all TM1 rules consist of?

  Response: A calculation statement consists of the area definition, leaf, consolidation, or string qualifier, formula, and a terminator.

- **Question**: What is the purpose of a TM1 rule area definition?

  Response: Each rule must have an area definition to define for Cognos TM1 which cell values to be calculated with a rule. Using areas you can specify which calculations apply to different parts of a cube.

- **Question**: What are the types of elements in TM1?

  Response: Cognos TM1 defines elements as either a numeric (`N:`), consolidation (`C:`), or a string (`S:`).

- **Question**: How do you signify the end of a TM1 rule statement?

  Response: All rules must end with a semicolon to terminate the statement.

- **Question**: Where do you associate rules that pull data from a source cube into a virtual cube?

  Response: They must be associated with the virtual cube.

- **Question**: Where do rules and feeders reside in a virtual cube and the cube it pulls data from?

  Response: When working with intercube rules, as in the case of virtual cubes, rule statements reside in the target (the virtual) cube, while feeder statements always reside in the source cube.

- **Question**: What rule function is used to reference data in another cube?

  Response: You must use the `DB` function. The `DB` function returns a value from a cube in a TM1 database.

- **Question**: What does the `DB` function return?

  Response: It returns a numeric value if used in a numeric expression and a string value if used in a string expression.

- **Question**: Can you use the TM1 Rules `DB` function more than once in the same TM1 rule?

  Response: The `DB` function can be used multiple times within a Cognos TM1 rule. This is referred to as nested `DB` functions.

- **Question**: How can you transfer data from a forecasting cube to a reporting cube?

  Response: You can create a hard cube and write a TI process to copy forecasts from each of the region cubes to the main cube to show your consolidated forecast or another solution. That solution may define the additional cube to consolidate all of the regions forecasts for reporting. So, instead of periodically copying data from the individual hard cubes to the consolidation cube, this cube can be a virtual cube using TM1 rules to reference or pull data from each of the source cubes.

- **Question**: If you create a virtual cube with `DB` functions to reference data in a hard cube, when will the data changes in the hard cube be visible in the virtual cube?

  Response: Using this method, information entered into any of the hard cubes would be available immediately in the consolidation or virtual cube.

- **Question**: What would be an example of using a virtual cube?

  Response: An example of using a virtual cube is entity consolidation.

- **Question**: Why might you create multiple virtual cubes for reporting in a TM1 application?

  Response: Some Cognos TM1 cubes may be very complicated, large, or have intensive rule calculations. In other examples, data required for a report may be sourced from multiple cubes. In these cases, specific end user reporting may become difficult (especially for the more casual TM1 user) or somewhat slow. Defining several specific virtual cubes—based upon unique views of the larger cube or cubes—can be a solution.

- **Question**: Define a lookup cube.

  Response: This is a sort of utility cube. Lookup cubes are cubes that you can set up and use to support other cubes within a TM1 application. These cubes are usually read-only or even made non-visible to the user and may contain calculations or reference data that are then pulled into other cubes using TM1 rules.

- **Question**: What is the purpose of a lookup cube?

  Response: Lookup cubes can be used to reference data in other TM1 cubes on the same TM1 Server.

- **Question**: When do you choose a lookup cube over a simple attribute?

  Response: If it is a single point translation (involves only one dimension), you would have to use an attribute. If the translation involves multiple points, you would use a lookup cube.

- **Question**: How should you name your lookup cubes?

  Response: Lookup cubes are not usually for end users. So, it is a good idea to name your lookup cubes with the Cognos TM1 control cube prefix `}`. You may name the lookup cube as, for example, `}AcctLkUp`. Using a consistent naming convention will make it easy to identify all lookup cubes in the TM1 instance.

- **Question**: What is the use of lookup cubes ?

  Response: For performance reasons, lookup cubes can be used to load data into a TM1 application without locking the cubes that the users see and use.

- **Question**: Which TM1 spreading method can use a lookup cube?

  Response: The data spreading method called Relative Proportional Spread can be used. This method spreads values to the children of a consolidation proportional to the children of a reference cell. The reference cell can be located in a lookup cube in the same TM1 instance.

8
Time Considerations

In this chapter, we will learn the importance and use of the time dimension in Cognos TM1 in regards to the current IBM Cognos TM1 Developer (Test COG-310) certification exam.

The current certification exam assigns a weightage of 3 percent to this topic.

The importance of time

Cognos TM1 applications are most often used to view, compare, and predict information over time. For the most part, information in TM1 will be:

- Trended over time
- Compared between different time periods
- Forecasted for future time periods

To support these requirements, most TM1 cubes will have time added as one (or more) dimension. Of all the considerations for deciding what dimensions should make up a TM1 cube, time is one of the (if not the most) important.

Most TM1 cubes will have at least one time dimension.

It is the purpose of time to allow analysis of past, present, and future information as well as to support the ability to predict the future (also known as forecasting).

When considering the concept of time in a TM1 cube you need to determine:

- The lowest level of time detail required
- If the data in your cube requires regular and consistent time cycles
- If the data in your cube requires any unusual, overlapping, or inconsistent time cycles
- If your cube requires any rolling time periods

Additionally it is important to consider:

- Will your cube be sharing data with other cubes already in your system?
- What will be the level of effort that may be required for the end user when accessing data?
- What will be the level of effort required to load data from external systems?
- What level of data is available from external systems now and in the future?
- What will be required for the application or system administrator to support a system based upon the way in which time is determined and structured within the application?

You must consider the following points:

- Flexibility when comparing data across multiple time periods
- Flexibility when creating new consolidated time periods in the future
- Maintenance effort required to update a time dimension(s) as new cycles are added
- Your rules—since the left hand side of a rule must be a fixed reference, you really don't want to have to maintain them every year because of your time dimension design

Granularity—the lowest level of time detail required

Granularity is the extent to which a system is broken down into small parts, either the system itself or its description or observation. It is the extent to which a larger entity is subdivided—Wikipedia.

The most common granularities for a time dimension are:

- Month
- Week
- Day

Month—two time dimensions

Cognos TM1 cubes that store data at the monthly level of detail may have one or two time dimensions. If you have two, this would mean that you will have one dimension for the year and one dimension for the month.

Why would you have both a year and a month dimension, in the same cube?

Some of the advantages of separating the year and month into two dimensions include:

- It is easier for year on year comparisons.
- It will require less maintenance for the system administrator requiring that only a single element be added to the year dimension once a year.
- It is easier to take advantage of TM1's relative data spreading

Disadvantages might include:

- It makes it difficult to view continuous time spans, for example, the previous 12 months.
- It limits the ability to easily keep year-month combinations.

> The Relative Proportional Spread method spreads values to the leaves (children) of a consolidation proportional to the leaves of a reference cell. The reference cell can be located in the cube from which you initiate spreading or in a separate cube. However, the reference cell must share the same consolidations as the cell from which you initiate spreading.

When using a two dimensional time model, a mindset might be for financial cubes, the year and month dimensions should follow the fiscal year of the business.

For example:

If the financial year is from July to June, you would set up the year dimension to have elements such as:

- 2009/2010
- 2010/2011
- 2011/2012

And so on.

You would set up the month dimension with elements running from July through June (as July, August, September, October, November, December, January, February, March, April, May, and June):

The month dimension may also include consolidated elements for:

- Year total
- Quarter totals
- Half-year totals

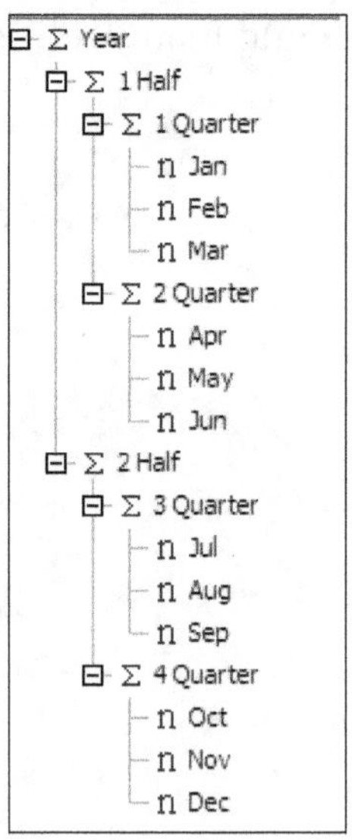

And optionally:

- Quarter to Date totals
- Year to Date totals

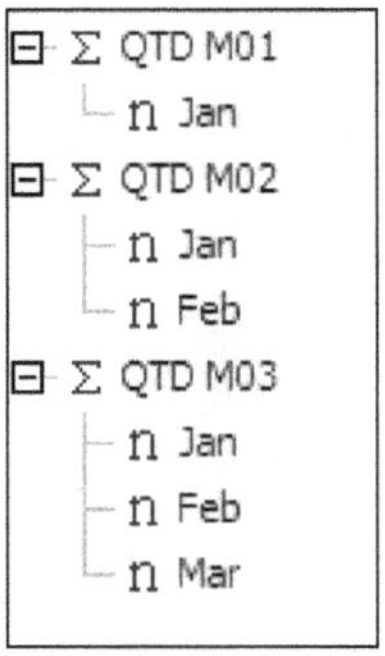

For non-financial cubes, the year and month dimensions may follow the structure as shown in the following screenshot:

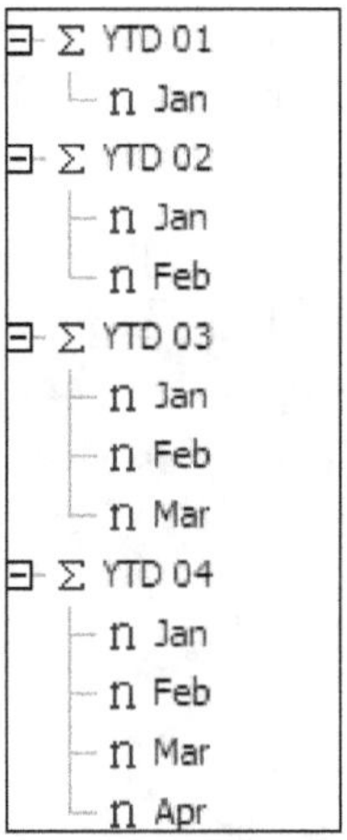

For financial cubes, it may be more appropriate that the year and month dimensions use a calendar year (with a set of months running from January to December):

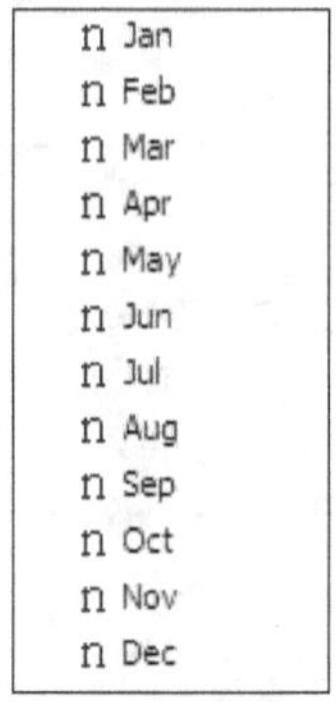

Month—one time dimension

In some situations, using a single time dimension may be more useful. For example, if the application requires rolling totals, it is easier to design these using consolidations in a single time dimension rather than by using rule calculations in a cube that has separate year and month dimensions. Single time dimensions can also make the development of some rule calculations easier (and easier to maintain) .

In cases where there is a requirement for rolling totals, time is usually modeled using consolidations in a single time dimension rather than by using other options such as rule calculations or having separate year and month dimensions. In fact, if forecasting is the purpose of the application, you will almost always see a single time dimension:

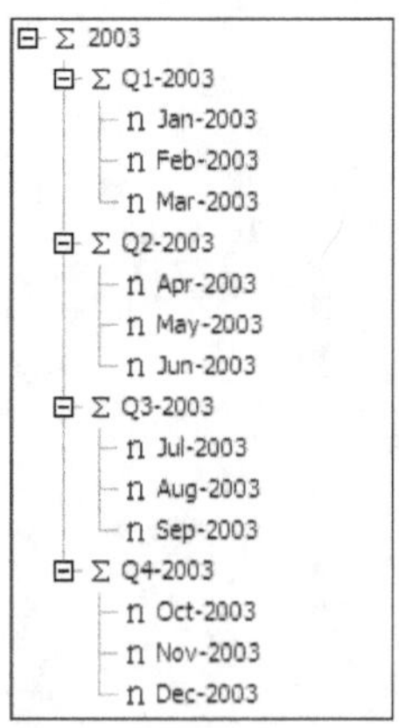

Single time dimensions usually:

- Support requirements like rolling forecasts.
- Make rule writing somewhat easier.
- May be easier to maintain by a system administrator (remember, Cognos TM1 does not have any built-in process to maintain dimensions (such as time). So, you will most likely need to provide some method to maintain this dimension.

Weeks

For cubes which must store weekly data design, the options you need to consider are as follows:

- Will the model follow a fiscal year or calendar year?
- A 365 or 366 day year does not contain an exact number of weeks!
- A 29, 30, or 31 days month does not contain an exact number of weeks!
- Using a 52 week system will eventually result in the days that are assigned to each year becoming more and more out of synchronization with the calendar.
- Weeks just do not fit neatly into a month!
- Leap years!
- Time pattern changes (if required) will affect the dimension design.

Days

For cube designs that store data at the daily level of detail, there are a number of different options such as using a three dimensional approach with year, week, and weekday.

> The maintenance using this approach is low; an additional year needs to be added to the year dimension once each year.

Lower than day detail

If your requirements for data are to capture and store data lower than a day (such as an hour or even a minute), an additional dimension should be added for that day's detail, along with appropriate aggregations or rollups.

Date format flexibility

One of the most commonly requested requirements for Cognos TM1 dates is the ability to select and display the date in a variety of formats. Although there are a number of supported TM1 functions (described later in this chapter) that you should be comfortable with, and most date format reporting requirements can be met using MS Excel formulas (or even simple macros), it is a very good idea to utilize TM1 attributes to support the (almost endless?) formats of date information.

In *Chapter 3, TurboIntegrator (TI)*, we explained the purpose and use of element attributes. It is a common practice to utilize element attributes to support the different date formats you may require in your TM1 application.

The planning sample model which is part of the Cognos TM1 installation offers a simple example of the use of element attributes to manipulate the value of dates. The `plan_time` dimension has the following attributes defined as type A (alias):

- `Time_ChineseSimplified`
- `Time_Spanish`
- `Time_Italian`
- `Time_Japanese`
- `Time_French`
- `Time_German`
- `Time_English`

These alias attributes can be used to select and view date values in different formats:

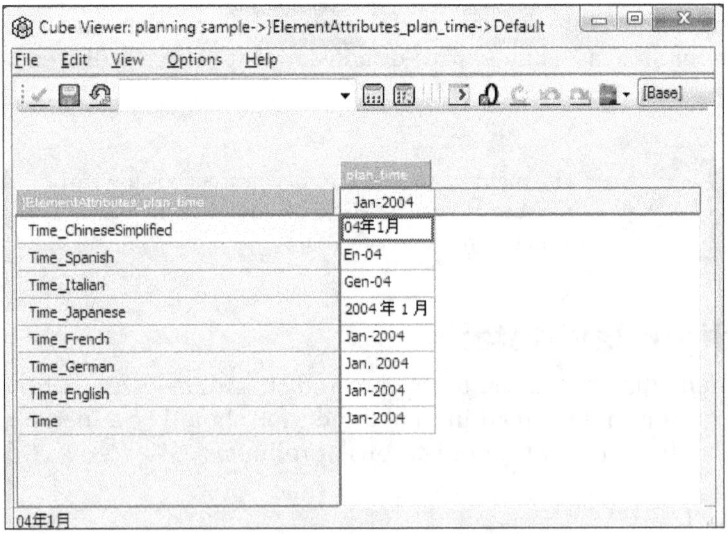

Aggregations

In *Chapter 3, TurboIntegrator (TI)*, we discussed TM1 aggregations. Some examples of aggregations relating to time are given in the next sections.

Time dimension aggregation examples

Some (but not all) of the more common time dimension consolidations used for aggregation are as follows:

- **Week**: Weeks may be consolidated simply by week number within the month. That is, Sep-WK1, Sep-WK2, Sep-WK3, and so on, which will rollup to Sep.
- **Month**: Of course, months may rollup to Quarter, Half-year, or directly to Year, depending upon your requirements. In addition, months may also rollup to fiscal years, QTD (quarter to date), and QTG (quarter to go) consolidations.
- **Quarter**: Quarters may rollup to Half-year or directly to Year—again, depending upon your requirements.
- **Year:** Most likely, Year will be a top-level consolidation. However, Years may also be grouped into alternative rollups depending upon your reporting needs. For example, all Years prior to an acquisition or other fundamental business event may rollup to Historic.
- **Fiscal Year**: Again, most likely, Fiscal Years will be a top-level consolidation. However, like YEARS, Fiscal Years may also be grouped into alternative rollups depending upon your reporting needs.
- **QTD**: QTD or **Quarter to Date** is a common aggregation or rollup that is used to include all periods from the start of a quarter to the current date. For example, this can be used to determine how a Quarter is shaping up.
- **QTG**: QTG or **Quarter to Go** is an aggregation or rollup that is used to include all periods from the current date to the end of the quarter.

Time dimension maintenance

Time dimensions, like any other dimension in IBM Cognos TM1, must first be initialized (created) and then maintained to keep the current dimension with the model's requirements. It is important to get a clear and accurate understanding of all of the reporting needs of the application or model owners before building the TM1 time dimension to ensure its usability.

Initialization

In some cases, the initialization of the model will include multiple forward years so that the time dimension maintenance will almost be non-existent for the foreseeable future. This means that the time dimension will include multiple dates past the current and next calendar and/or fiscal years. This is referred to as **future proofing** the time dimension.

In other cases, it may be important to only include currently used dates to simplify use of the model, enhance readability, or discourage possible errors in reporting. In these cases, a method needs to be defined to allow the addition (or removal) of dates now needed (or no longer needed) within the model.

Maintenance—manual

Depending upon the size of the application and/or number of users (and other factors), it may be completely acceptable for a TM1 Administrator to manually modify this dimension using the TM1 Dimension Editor.

In *Chapter 3, TurboIntegrator (TI)*, we discussed TM1 dimension maintenance. For all TM1 dimensions, the method of maintaining time dimensions must be considered.

Maintenance—automated

In other situations, a TI process may accept appropriate parameters and then update the time dimension.

Maintenance—in general

In any case, all applications deserve a documented and tested approach to maintain the model's time dimension.

Date and time Rules functions

The following Cognos TM1 functions deal with dates and times and therefore, I believe that they are important enough to warrant a quick review:

- `DATE`
- `DATES`
- `DAY`
- `DAYNO`

- MONTH
- NOW
- TIME
- TIMST
- TMIVL
- TODAY
- YEAR

Please note that although all of the mentioned functions are TM1 RULES functions, each can be used within a TI process as well.

DATE

The DATE function returns a date string like YY-MM-DD for a given serial number. Good to know because the function NOW will return us a serial number!

```
Foo=DATE(NOW, 1);
# --- will return a string of 'YYYY-MM-DD"
```

DATES

DATES is a little more practical (in my opinion). It takes a numeric value for a given year, month, and day and returns a string in a similar format:

```
Foo=DATES(2012,12,2);
# --- will return a string of "YYYY-MM-DD"
```

DAY

DAY returns a numeric value for the day in a given date string:

```
Foo=DAY('02-05-25');
# --- will return 25
```

DAYNO

`DAYNO` is reverse of `DAY`, the `DAYNO` function returns the serial date number corresponding to a given date string:

```
Foo=DAYNO('98-03-09');
# --- will return 13947.
```

MONTH

To easily pull the month from a date string, the `MONTH` function returns a numeric value for the month in a given date string:

```
Foo=MONTH('98-03-09');
# --- will return 3
```

NOW

This function can be used to return the current date and time from the system clock. Keep in mind though, that it returns the date/time in a serial number format.

```
NOW;
```

TIME

`TIME` is a "sister" to `NOW`, the `TIME` function returns a string, in `HH:MM` format, representing the system time on the TM1 Server:

```
TIME;
```

TIMST

The `TIMST` function takes a date/time serial number and returns a formatted date/time string based upon the format parameter's value which you provide. You can also pass an optional parameter called extended years:

```
FOO=TIMST(NOW, '\M \D, \Y');
# --- will return "DEC 27, 2011"
```

ExtendedYears

This optional Boolean parameter specifies whether the function returns a date falling within the range 1960 - 2059 or 1960 - 9999.

If `ExtendedYears` is true, the function returns a date falling within the range of January 1, 1960 and December 31, 9999. Serial date `0` corresponds to January 1, 1960 and serial date `2936549` corresponds to December 31, 9999.

If `ExtendedYears` is false, or if this optional argument is omitted from the `TIMVL` function, the function returns a date falling within the range January 1, 1960 and December 31, 2059. Serial date `0` corresponds to January 1, 1960 and serial date `36524` corresponds to December 31, 2059.

If `ExtendedYears` is false or is omitted and you specify a serial date greater than `36524`, the serial date used by the function is determined by the formula `n - 36525`. For example, if you specify a serial date of `36530`, then the formula is `36530 - 36525` = 5. In this case, `TIMVL` uses `5` as the serial date and returns the date January 6, 1960.

TIMVL

The `TIMVL` function is a lot like the `TIMST` function. It accepts a date/time serial number and two parameters, but returns the numeric value of a component (year, month, and so on) of a date/time value.

```
Foo=TIMVL(NOW, 'Y');
# --- will return "2011"
```

TODAY

This function has an optional parameter to define the resulting format. No parameter given will return a two digit year within the string (`YY-MM-DD`) and a parameter of `1` will return a four digit year within the string (`YYYY-MM-DD`):

```
Foo=TODAY;
# --- will return "11-12-27"
```

YEAR

The `YEAR` function takes a date string and returns the numeric year in the string:

```
YEAR('2012-12-12');
# --- will return 12
```

Summary

In this chapter, we have discussed the basics of the time dimension in Cognos TM1 focusing on what you need to know and be comfortable with before taking the current IBM Cognos TM1 Developer (Test COG-310) certification exam. We have also looked at some practical examples for defining time with a TM1 application.

Two minute drill

There are some important points that you must know:

- Cognos TM1 applications will most often be used to view, compare, and predict information over time.
- Of all the considerations for deciding what dimensions should make up a TM1 cube, time is one of the (if not the most) important.
- The vast majority of TM1 cubes will have at least one time dimension.
- Granularity is the lowest level of time detail required.
- The most common granularities for a time dimension are Month, Week, and Day.
- Cognos TM1 cubes that store data at the monthly level of detail may have one or two time dimensions.
- When using a two dimensional time model, a rule of thumb might be for financial cubes such as **general ledger** (**GL**).
- The year and month dimensions should conform to the financial year of the business.
- A common month dimension may also include consolidated elements for Year totals, Quarter totals, and Half-year totals.
- Optional time consolidations may include Quarter to Date and Year to Date rollups.
- Time dimensions in TM1 should consider if cubes will be sharing data with other cubes already in your system.
- Time dimensions in TM1 should consider what will be the level of effort that may be required for the end user when accessing data.
- Time dimensions in TM1 should consider rules—since the left hand side of a rule must be a fixed reference, you really don't want to have to maintain them every year because of your time dimension design.

- The advantages of separating year and month into two dimensions include:
    - It is easier for year on year comparisons.
    - It will require less maintenance for the system administrator requiring that only a single element be added to the year dimension once a year.
    - It is easier to take advantage of TM1's relative data spreading.
- In some circumstances using a single time dimension is more useful.
- Single time dimensions can also make the development of some rule calculations more straightforward.
- For cubes that must store weekly information, the best approach may be to have two time dimensions.
- Using a 52 week system will eventually result in the days that are assigned to each year becoming more and more out of synchronization with the calendar year as years pass.
- It is a very good idea to utilize TM1 attributes to support the formats of date information.
- In addition to defining an element's type (numeric, consolidation, or string), elements can have attributes defined for them.
- Time dimensions, like any other dimension in IBM Cognos TM1, must first be initialized (created) and then maintained to keep current with the model's requirements.
- Depending upon the size of the application and/or number of users (and other factors), it may be completely acceptable for a TM1 Administrator to manually modify this dimension using the TM1 Dimension Editor.
- The following Cognos TM1 functions deal with dates and times and therefore, I believe that they are important enough to warrant a quick review:
    - `DATE`
    - `DATES`
    - `DAY`
    - `DAYNO`
    - `MONTH`
    - `NOW`
    - `TIME`
    - `TIMST`
    - `TMIVL`

    - TODAY
    - YEAR

- Using a single time dimension allows the creation of any possible grouping of individual dates. However, it requires the most amount of maintenance and affords the least amount of flexibility when performing period on period comparisons.

Self-test

- **Question**: For the most part, what will be the information in TM1?

  Response: The information in TM1 will be trended over time, compared between different time periods, and forecasted for future time periods.

- **Question**: To support these requirements, how will most TM1 cubes have time added?

  Response: The TM1 cubes will have time added as one (or more) dimension.

- **Question**: Of all the considerations for deciding what dimensions should make up a TM1 cube, what may be the most important?

  Response: Time is one of the (if not the most) important considerations.

- **Question**: What is the role of the time dimension?

  Response: The role of the time dimension is to allow the analysis of past, present, and future information as well as to support the ability to predict the future (also known as forecasting).

- **Question**: When considering the concept of time in a TM1 cube, what do you need to determine?

  Response: You need to determine the lowest level of time detail required, if the data in your cube requires regular and consistent time cycles, if the data in your cube requires any unusual, overlapping, or inconsistent time cycles, and if your cube will require any rolling time periods.

- **Question**: What are the four basic types of cubes in Cognos TM1?

  Response: Standard cubes, control cubes, virtual cubes, and lookup cubes.

- **Question**: Name three important considerations when adding `TIME` to your cube design.

  Response: The considerations are as follows:

  - Will your cube be sharing data with other cubes already in your system?
  - What will be the level of effort that may be required for the end user when accessing data?
  - What will be the level of effort required to load data from external systems?

- **Question**: In respect to maintaining `TIME` in your model, what must be considered?

  Response: You must consider flexibility when comparing data across multiple time periods, flexibility when creating new consolidated time periods in the future, the maintenance effort required to update time dimension(s) as new cycles are added, and your rules—since the left hand side of a rule must be a fixed reference, you really don't want to have to maintain them every year because of your time dimension design.

- **Question**: What is granularity?

  Response: Granularity is the lowest level of time detail required.

- **Question**: What are the most common granularities for a time dimension?

  Response: Month, Week, and Day.

- **Question**: Cognos TM1 cubes that store data at the monthly level of detail may have one or two time dimensions. If you have two, what would this mean?

  Response: It would mean that you have one dimension for the year and one dimension for the month.

- **Question**: Why would you have both a year and a month dimension, in the same cube?

  Response: It is easier for year on year comparisons, it will require less maintenance for the system administrator, requiring that only a single element needs to be added to the year dimension once a year, and it is easier to take advantage of TM1's relative data spreading.

- **Question**: Describe a rule of thumb when using a two dimensional time model.

  Response: A rule might be that the year and month dimensions should conform to the financial year of the business.

- **Question**: What may the consolidated elements of the month dimension also include?

  Response: Year totals, Quarter totals, Half-year totals, and optionally Quarter to Date totals and Year to Date totals.

- **Question**: For non-financial cubes, what should the year and month dimensions use to make the structure more appropriate?

  Response: A calendar year (with a set of months running from January to December).

- **Question**: When can using a single time dimension be more useful?

  Response: If the application requires rolling totals for example, it is easier to model these using consolidations in a single time dimension rather than using rule calculations in a cube that has separate year and month dimensions.

- **Question**: What may be an advantage of using a single time dimension?

  Response: Single time dimensions may also make the development of some rule calculations more straightforward.

- **Question**: In the case where there is a requirement for rolling totals, how is time usually modeled?

  Response: Time is usually modeled using consolidations in a single time dimension rather than using other options such as rule calculations or having separate year and month dimensions.

- **Question**: Name some characteristics of a single time dimension.

  Response: Support requirements such as rolling forecasts make rule writing somewhat easier, and may be easier to maintain by a system administrator.

- **Question**: For cubes that must store weekly information the best approach may be to have two time dimensions. Which would be these dimensions?

  Response: One dimension for year and one dimension for week.

- **Question**: What challenges does the use of a week dimension create?

  Response: A 365 or 366 day year does not contain an exact number of weeks and a 29, 30, or 31 days month does not contain an exact number of weeks.

- **Question**: What will using a 52 week system result in?

  Response: The days that are assigned to each year becoming more and more out of synchronization with the calendar year as years pass.

- **Question**: How should week dimensions be set up?

  Response: With 53 weeks, not 52.

- **Question**: If for any reason the time pattern needs to change from year to year, what should be considered?

  Response: Then a single time dimension will be more appropriate.

- **Question**: How are single week-based time dimensions usually built?

  Response: The single week-based dimensions are based upon a business calendar with the appropriate number of weeks rolling up to each month.

- **Question**: What does using a single time dimension allow?

  Response: It allows the creation of any possible grouping of individual dates. However, it requires the most amount of maintenance and affords the least amount of flexibility when performing period on period comparisons.

- **Question**: If data needs to be stored at a lower level of detail than day, what is normally required?

  Response: Then an additional dimension should be added for the day part.

- **Question**: What is one of the most commonly requested requirements for Cognos TM1 dates?

  Response: The ability to select and display the date in a variety of formats.

- **Question**: Although there are a number of supported TM1 functions that you should be comfortable with, what are some alternative methods for formatting TM1 dates?

  Response: Most date format reporting requirements can be met using MS Excel formulas.

- **Question**: In addition to defining an element's type, what can elements have defined for them?

  Response: Elements can have attributes defined for them. If elements identify data in a cube, then think of the element attributes as describing the elements themselves.

- **Question**: What is the method for formatting dates in TM1?

  Response: Attributes with alternative date formats can help in doing data analysis by making it easier to search for and locate a particular date.

- **Question**: What could be the advantage of using element attributes?

  Response: You can select elements by attribute value in the Subset Editor. You can also display element names in TM1 windows using their aliases.

- **Question**: What are some (but not all) of the common time dimension consolidations used for aggregation to be aware of?

  Response: Week, Month, Quarter, Year, Fiscal Year, QTD, and QTG.

- **Question**: In most cases, the initialization of the model will include multiple forward years so that the time dimension maintenance will almost be non-existent for the foreseeable future. What does this mean?

  Response: This means that the time dimension will include multiple dates past the current and next calendar and/or fiscal years. This is referred to as future proofing the time dimension.

- **Question**: In some cases, it may be important to only include currently used or active dates in the time dimension. Why?

  Response: Dates can simplify the use of the model enhance readability or discourage possible errors in reporting. In these cases, a method needs to be defined to allow the addition (or removal) of dates which is currently needed (or no longer needed) within the model.

- **Question**: When may it be completely acceptable for a TM1 Administrator to manually modify a time dimension using the TM1 Dimension Editor?

  Response: Depending upon the size of the application and/or number of users (and other factors).

- **Question**: What is another method for maintaining a TM1 time dimension?

  Response: In some situations a TI process may be useful to accept appropriate parameters and then update the time dimension.

- **Question**: Name some Cognos TM1 functions that deal with dates and times.

  Response: `DATE`, `DATES`, `DAY`, `DAYNO`, `MONTH`, `NOW`, `TIME`, `TIMST`, `TMIVL`, `TODAY`, and `YEAR`.

9
Data Presentation and Reporting

In this chapter, we will identify techniques for data presenting and reporting in a TM1 application, with regards to the current IBM Cognos TM1 Developer (Test COG-310) certification exam.

The current certification exam assigns a weightage of 3 percent to this topic.

The ability to browse for the present information stored within a TM1 application is required for the certification exam. However, it is also a valuable skill for every level of TM1 user or developer.

Basic data browsing in TM1

This section will discuss the methods for browsing data in TM1 cubes by using either Cube Viewer or In-Spreadsheet Browser.

Cube Viewer

Cube Viewer does not require programming to implement. It works for all cubes in a TM1 instance for which the logged-in user has access. The following steps can be followed to browse data in the Cube Viewer:

1. Open TM1 Server Explorer.
2. In the **Tree** pane, select the cube you want to browse.

3. Click on the cube and select **Browse...**:

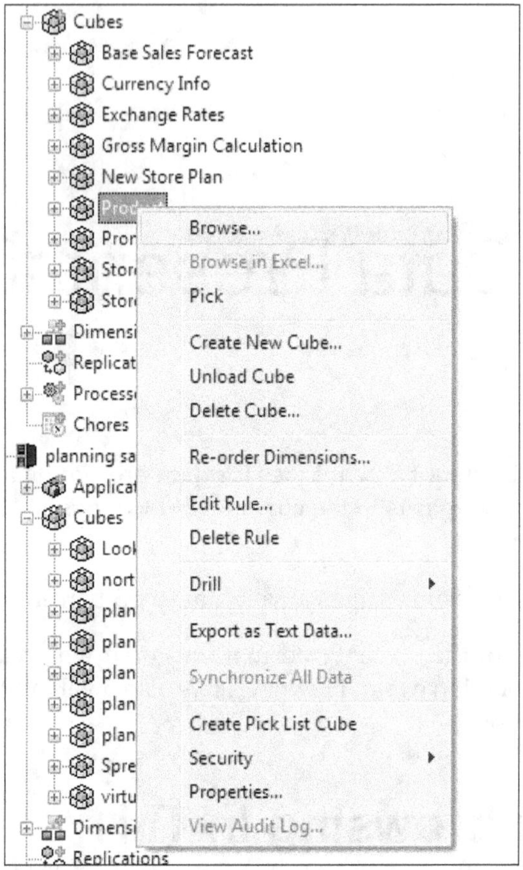

4. The Cube Viewer window opens with the cube's system default view.
5. Press *F9* or click on **Recalculate** to display the cell values.

With mouse clicks and drags-and-drops, the cube view of the data can be easily customized to meet your requirements.

In-Spreadsheet Browser

In-Spreadsheet Browser (**ISB**) does not require any programming to use. However, you may want to configure what browsing method TM1 will use as the default browser – the Cube Viewer or the In-Spreadsheet Browser.

[When you double-click on a cube or view in Server Explorer, that cube or view opens in Cube Viewer. If you prefer browsing data in Excel spreadsheets, you can set In-Spreadsheet Browser as your default browser.]

To access data using this tool the following steps should be followed:

1. Open Server Explorer.
2. In the **Tree** pane, select the cube you want to browse.
3. Click on the cube and select **Browse in Excel**.

[This option is not available if you are using TM1 Architect.]

Modifying your view of data

From TM1 Cube Viewer, the display or view of information can easily be rearranged or changed. To do this, Cube Viewer allows a user to perform the following:

- Stack dimensions to see more detail along the columns or rows of a view
- Drill down on the consolidated elements displayed in the view to see the underlying detail
- Change the title dimension elements in the view to access a completely different view of the cube data
- Drill-through the view to detailed data (if a drill process and rule is set up as described in *Chapter 6, Drill-through*)

Stacking a title dimension as a row dimension

To stack a title dimension as a row dimension in Cube Viewer, you can click on the element name in the title dimension and drag that element name to the right or left of a row dimension name.

Stacking a title dimension as a column dimension

To stack a title dimension as a column dimension in Cube Viewer, you can click on the element name in the title dimension and drag that element name to the right or left of a column dimension name.

Drilling down through consolidations

In Cube Viewer, a plus sign (+), next to an element name, identifies the element as a consolidation. To view the underlying detail, click on **+**, and to hide the underlying detail, click on the minus sign (**-**).

Changing title elements in Cube Viewer

To change title elements displayed in Cube Viewer, click on the element name arrow, select an element, and press *F9*.

Drilling through to detailed data

To access detailed level data for a selected cell of data in Cube Viewer, a drill TI process and drill association rule must be implemented (this process was described in *Chapter 6, Drill-through*).

Saving the view

Once you have a view created and customized to your requirements, you can save that view to quickly access it in the future. This view can be saved as the default for the cube. That means that when you double-click on that cube within TM1 Server Explorer, this view would be the initially displayed data.

To save a view from Cube Viewer, you can click on **File** and then select **Save**. TM1 will prompt you with the **TM1 Save View** dialog. This dialog allows you to:

- Set this view as the cube's default view (only one default view per cube is allowed)
- Save the view as a private or public view
- Provide a name for the view

TM1 Server Explorer displays view names beneath the cube with which they are associated. Icons will indicate whether a save view is a public view or a private view.

Formatting view cells

The most common features provided by TM1 to format data displayed in a cube view are:

- Zero suppression
- Cell formatting
- Column orientations

Zero suppression

You can turn off rows and/or columns that are zero. The steps to accomplish this are as follows:

For row suppression, click on **Options** | **Suppress Zeroes On Rows**:

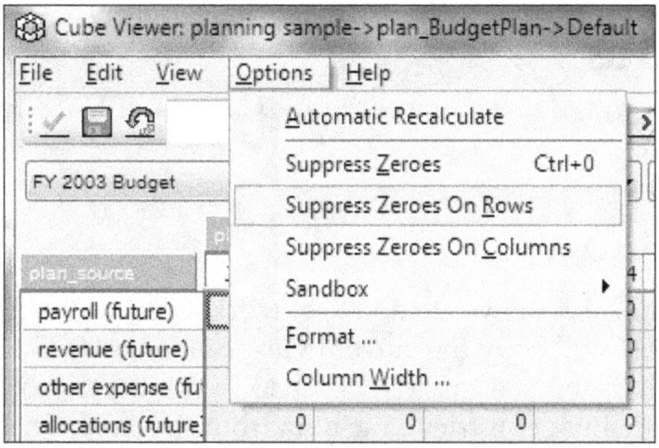

For column suppression, click on **Options** | **Suppress Zeroes On Columns**:

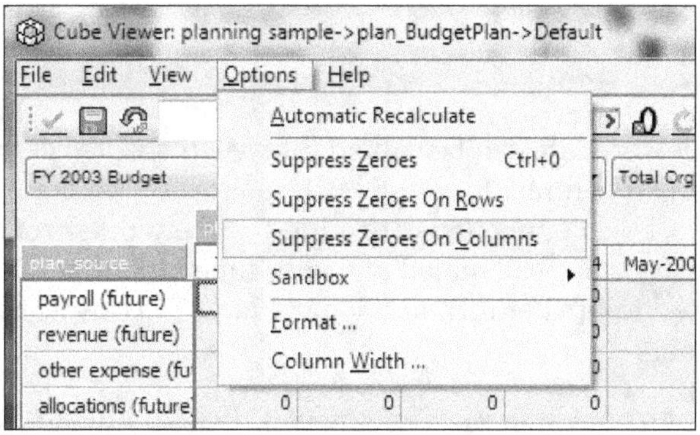

Cell formatting

To customize the display of data within a cube view cell, the Format attribute can be used. The Format attribute is a special type of element attribute that determines how data is displayed. The value of the format attribute can be applied to column elements, row elements, or title elements.

An even more basic method of formatting cube views is to set view options directly within Cube Viewer itself.

Column orientations

Column elements are displayed left to right by default in TM1. You may change it from right to left by clicking on the menu option **Layout Right to Left** (or **Layout Left to Right**, depending upon the current view).

Worksheets

From TM1 Cube Viewer, data can be sliced into Microsoft Excel for analysis and further presentation.

Slicing a view

To slice a view from Cube Viewer to an Excel worksheet, you can click on **File** and then select **Slice**. TM1 will copy the current view into a new MS Excel workbook. Sliced views are still connected to TM1, because TM1 adds the appropriate TM1 functions to the worksheet to retrieve the data from the cube. The workbook can be saved, reopened later, and, as long as you are logged into the TM1 instance, the latest cube data can be viewed from within the workbook. All of the cell formatting available in MS Excel can be used to further format the data.

Snapshots

From TM1 Cube Viewer, data can be copied into Microsoft Excel for analysis and further presentation. In contrast to the slice, the snapshot is a copy of the data at that moment in time. No TM1 connections are added to the worksheet and data cannot be automatically refreshed or recalculated at a later time but all of the cell formatting in MS Excel can be used to further format the data. Non-TM1 users can view and work with the information.

To create a snapshot from Cube Viewer, you can click on **File** and then select **Snapshot**.

Active Forms

Active Forms let you view (and update) cube data directly in Excel whenever you are connected to the server on which the cube data resides. The exciting thing about Active Forms is that these reports retain the ability to expand and collapse row dimension consolidations in TM1 views while allowing you to use native Excel features and functions to create complex reports. This in effect means that if the set of data changes within TM1, Active Form reports will automatically have access to the new view of the data without requiring any changes or reprogramming.

Active Forms support most features available in Cube Viewer, including selectable title dimensions, stacked row and column dimensions, expandable/collapsible consolidations (rows only), zero suppression (rows only), drill-through, filtering, and data spreading.

TM1 Active Forms are supported in TM1 Web, if an Active Form is added to TM1 applications, that form can be accessed and used in TM1 Web.

There are a special groups of TM1 worksheet functions that are used for the support of Active Forms. These groups include:

- `TM1RptView`
- `TM1RptTitle`
- `TM1RptRow`
- `TM1RptFilter`
- `TM1RptElLev`
- `TM1RptElIsExpanded`
- `TM1RptElIsConsolidated`

The most basic method of creating an Active Form report is by using Cube Viewer. From the menu, you can click on **File** and then select **Active Form**.

Additionally, in (almost) any empty cell in any Excel worksheet, you can insert a new Active Form by right-clicking on the cell and selecting **Active Form**. Then you can select **Insert Active Form** (generally the rule is that you may have trouble inserting a new Active Form into a worksheet that already contains an Active Form—depending upon where you try to insert it).

Refreshing and recalculating

Once you have saved an Active Form, you can refresh the data displayed in it by pressing *F9*. Additionally, you also have the option to rebuild the current worksheet or current workbook by clicking on **Active Form** and then selecting **Rebuild Current Sheet** (or **Rebuild Current Workbook**).

Deleting an Active Form

To remove an Active Form from a worksheet, you must click in the data area of an Active Form and then click on **Active Form** | **Delete**. Unfortunately (or fortunately), when you delete an Active Form from a worksheet, only the data area is removed from the worksheet. The column headings, title elements, and formatting area remain in the worksheet.

Active Forms and special formatting

You will find that you can format Active Forms in a variety of ways. Similar to Cube Viewer, you can use zero suppression, holding and spreading, drilling, edited subsets, static lists, changing of the title element, dependent sectioning, and column insertion.

A quick summary of these features is available in the TM1 Help documentation:

- **Supressing zero values**: You can selectively suppress or display rows containing only zero values in an Active Form.
- **Spreading and holding data**: All data spreading and holding operations are fully supported within Active Forms.
- **Drill**: The ability to drill-to related data displayed in an Active Form is supported (drill processes and rules must first be set up).
- **Editing of the row subsets used**: The row subset for an Active Form is defined by the `TM1RptRow` function and can be changed.
- **Static lists**: The row subset within an Active Form can be saved as a static list by clicking on **Active Form** and then selecting **Save Row Elements as Static List**.
- **Changing the title element**: You can access a completely different view of cube data in the Active Form by double clicking a title element in the Active Form, then selecting a new element and clicking on **OK**.

- **Inserting a dependent section**: An Active Form can be split into multiple sections to access additional data. An additional Active Section would use the same column and title dimensions as the parent Active Form with which it is associated, but has unique row elements.
- **Insertion of columns**: You can insert a column within an Active Form directly within the Active Form, to the left of the Active Form, or to the right of the Active Form.

Formatting Active Forms

Active Form formatting is defined directly in the worksheet containing the form. There are default formats set by TM1 but they can be changed.

Active Form formatting is defined via a format range which is hidden within the Active Form worksheet. This hidden range is revealed by clicking on **Active Form** and then selecting **Show Format Area**.

Active Form default formatting

Active Forms must have the default formatting defined in rows 1 to 8 where row 1 will always have the **Begin Format Range** label and row 8 will always have the **End Format Range** label:

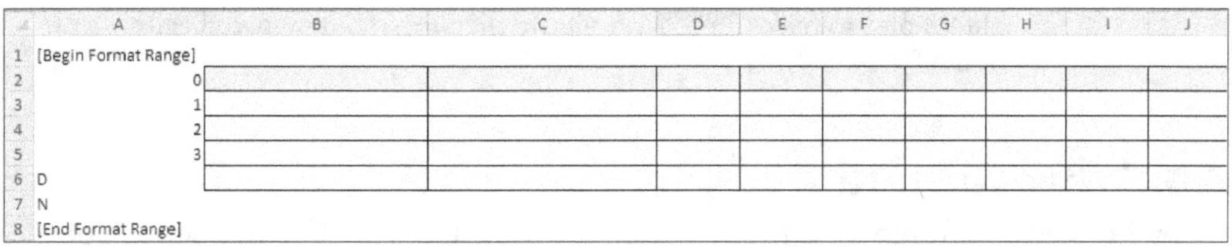

With the formatting range, rows 2 through 7 will be the actual formatting definitions.

Column A (in rows 2 through 7) contains the **Format Definition** labels used to format the Active Form. These labels can be numbers, letters, or string values. For each data row in the Active Form, column A contains a value that determines which format definition should be applied to the row.

Column B (in rows 2 through 7) defines the formatting for the row elements in the Active Form.

Column C defines the formatting for the data cells in the Active form.

Modifying default formatting

The Active Form uses the defined formatting range (described above) for all of the formatting within the Active Form. To change the formatting from what TM1 provided as a default format, you can apply all standard cell formats available in the **Excel Format Cells** dialog box.

Any changes that you make in the format range of an active form will be applied to the worksheet when you save and recalculate that form.

Even though the formatting range for an Active Form is initially defined in rows 2 through 7, you can create multiple additional format definitions and insert them between the **Begin Format Range** and **End Format Range** labels of the Active Form:

1. Click on the **End Format Range** label.
2. From the **Excel Insert** menu, click on **Row**.
3. Use the **Excel Format Cells** dialog box to apply formatting to the cells in the new formatting row.
4. In column A, assign a unique format definition label to the formatting row.

> **Documentation**
>
> Anything you enter in a formatting row is ignored. So, you can enter notes to make it easy to identify the format of any given cell in the format range.

Applying formatting

If you defined an additional format, column A of the first row in your Active Form must contain a function that resolves to one of the format definition labels in the format range.

You cannot use hardcoded values while specifying format definition labels in column A, as the format definition label in the first row will be automatically copied to all other rows in the form, overwriting the hardcoded values.

Active Form limitations

There are some limitations with using Active Forms:

- Worksheet names cannot include a dash (-) character.
- Merging cells in an Active Form always requires a rebuild of the worksheet or workbook.
- Active Forms require at least one row dimension.

TM1 reports

TM1 Print Report Wizard can be used to print reports or to save reports as Excel or PDF documents.

TM1 reports must be created from a TM1 slice (described earlier in this chapter). From there, TM1 reports utilize a Report Generation Wizard to:

- Select the worksheets to be included in the report
- Select the title dimensions and subsets for the report
- Select workbook print options
- Select a print destination for the report (printer, Excel file, or PDF file)
- Save the report settings

TM1 Print Report Wizard

To use the reporting wizard, from the menu bar, click on **TM1**, then select the **Print Report** option. From the **Print Report Wizard** dialog, you can select the desired options and click on **Next** to step through and set up all of the report options and then click on **Finish**.

Selecting the sheets

You can use TM1 Print Report Wizard to select any (or all) of the worksheets from the current Excel workbook to include in your report. In the wizard, you can select the checkbox of the worksheet that you want to include in the report or you can click on **Select All** to include all of the worksheets in the current workbook in the report.

Selecting the title dimensions

TM1 Print Report Wizard will list the sheet name and title dimensions of your slice. You can select the title dimensions to be included in the report by selecting and moving them from the **Available Title Dimensions** list to the **Selected Title Dimensions** list.

Selecting workbook print options

TM1 Print Report Wizard can be used to control the number and grouping of worksheets in the report. You can perform the following operations:

- **Print a single workbook or print multiple workbooks**: You can use TM1 Print Report Wizard to print a single workbook or even multiple workbooks.
- **Selecting a print destination**: The final step in using TM1 Print Report Wizard to create a report is to select a print destination of a printer, Excel file, or PDF file. Printing options available include the printer name, number of copies, print to file, and collate.
- **Saving the TM1 report as an Excel or PDF document**: You can select the **Save as Excel Files** or **Save as PDF Files** option on third screen of the TM1 Print Report Wizard to save the report in the desired format.

For these options you can provide the following:

1. Generate a new workbook for each title.
2. Generate a file name for Excel or PDF.
3. Generate a directory name or location in which to save the output file(s).
4. For Excel output files, specify if the generated report will include TM1 formulas to access TM1 data in the future.

TM1 Web

TM1 Web allows access to the cube data, provides the ability to view and edit via Excel reports, drill, pivot, select, and filter the TM1 data, cube data sourced charts, and even some TM1 Server Administrator tasks.

TM1 Web consists of the **Navigation** pane on the left and the **Content** pane on the right. The **Navigation** pane contains a list of available TM1 applications, views, and a list of server object properties. TM1 Web's **Content** pane displays the cube views and websheets to which you have access.

TM1 Web allows access to TM1 data and the ability to present TM1 data using TM1 Websheets, TM1 Web Cube Viewer, and TM1 Charts.

TM1 Websheets

By publishing an Excel worksheet from TM1 to an application folder, other users can view the worksheet by using a Web browser. It should be understood that the websheet version of the Excel sheet will have various visual differences but it does support the following Excel features:

- Hiding columns
- Conditional formatting
- Hyperlinking
- Freeze panes
- Cell protection

In this websheet a user can:

- Enter data in cells to which they have write access
- Use the data spreading feature of TM1
- Drill to relational tables or other cubes
- View Excel charts
- Manipulate title element subsets in the Subset Editor

TM1 Web Cube Viewer

Earlier in this chapter, we reviewed accessing and presenting data using TM1 Cube Viewer. To utilize Cube Viewer within TM1 Web you can:

- Log in to TM1 Web and open **Views** in the **Navigation** pane
- Expand the cube views that you are interested in and click on the view that you wish to access

TM1 Web Cube Viewer can be reconfigured in various ways to support your needs. You can expand and collapse consolidations, pivot dimensions, hide dimensions, filter view data, edit subsets, and drill-through to associated data.

Creating a new TM1 Web cube view

To create a new TM1 Web cube view, you can use the TM1 Web View Builder Wizard. This wizard helps you to define the location of dimensions in the view, select the elements to be used in the view, and save the view as a private view on the server.

TM1 Charts

TM1 Web supports a variety of customizable chart types. To view cube data in TM1 Web in chart format, you can click on **View Chart**, **View Chart and Grid**, or **View Grid from the toolbar**.

From the TM1 Web chart display, you can click on **Chart Properties** to change the chart type, colors, legend, and 3D view elements.

Custom display formats

In *Chapter 2, Dimensions and Cubes*, we reviewed element attributes and the Format attribute. Again, to revisit, this attribute allows the definition of a number of formats for numbers, dates, times, and strings. If you right-click on a dimension, click on **Edit Element Attributes**, and then click on the cell at the intersection of the **Format** column and the element for which you want to define a display format, TM1 will allow you to select a standard format for that element or define your own. These formats will be applied to all cells in the defined data intersection.

Summary

In this chapter, we have discussed the basics of data access, presentation, and reporting in Cognos TM1, focusing on what you will need to know and be comfortable with before taking the current IBM Cognos TM1 Developer (Test COG-310) certification exam.

Two minute drill

There are some important points about data presentation and reporting:

- The most basic methods for browsing data in TM1 cubes are by using either Cube Viewer or In-Spreadsheet Browser.
- In-Spreadsheet Browser (ISB) does not require programming to implement. However, it may be up to you to configure what browsing method TM1 will use as the default browser—Cube Viewer or In-Spreadsheet Browser.
- When you double-click on a cube or view in Server Explorer, that cube or view opens in Cube Viewer. If you prefer browsing data in Excel spreadsheets, you can set In-Spreadsheet Browser as your default browser.

- To stack title dimensions as a row dimension in Cube Viewer, you can click on the element name in the title dimension and drag that element name to the right or left of a row dimension name.
- To stack title dimensions as a column dimension in Cube Viewer you can click on the element name in the title dimension and drag that element name to the right or left of a column dimension name.
- In Cube Viewer, a plus sign (+) next to an element name identifies the element as a consolidation. To view the underlying detail, click on **+**, to hide the underlying detail, click on the minus sign (**-**).
- To change title elements displayed in Cube Viewer, click on an element name arrow, select an element, and press *F9*.
- To save a view from Cube Viewer click on **File** and then select **Save**.
- TM1 Server Explorer displays view names beneath the cube with which they are associated.
- To customize the display of data within a cube view cell, the Format attribute can be used.
- The Format attribute is a special type of element attribute that determines how data is displayed.
- To slice a view from Cube Viewer to an Excel worksheet, click on **File** and then select **Slice**.
- To create a snapshot from Cube Viewer, click on **File** and then select **Snapshot**.
- Active Forms let you view (and update) cube data directly in Excel whenever you are connected to the server on which the cube data resides.
- Active Forms support most features available in Cube Viewer, including selectable title dimensions, stacked row and column dimensions, expandable/collapsible consolidations (rows only), zero suppression (rows only), drill-through, filtering, and data spreading.
- TM1 Active Forms are supported in TM1 Web, if an Active Form is added to TM1 Applications, that form can be accessed and used in TM1 Web.
- Once you have saved an Active Form, you can refresh the data displayed in it by pressing *F9*.
- To remove an Active Form from a worksheet, you must click in the data area of an Active Form and then click on **Active Form | Delete**.

- Active Form formatting is defined via a format range which is hidden within the Active Form worksheet. This hidden range is revealed by clicking on **Active Form** and then selecting **Show Format Area**.
- Active Forms must have the default formatting defined in rows 1 to 8 where row 1 will always have the **Begin Format Range** label and row 8 will always have the **End Format Range** label.
- All changes made in the format range are applied to all cells in the Active Forms worksheets that use the corresponding format definition updated when you recalculate the form.
- If you have defined an additional format, column A of the first row in your Active Form must contain a function that resolves to one of the format definition labels in the format range.
- TM1 Print Report Wizard can be used to print reports or save reports as Excel or PDF documents.
- TM1 reports must be created from a TM1 slice (described earlier in this chapter).
- To use the reporting wizard, from the menu bar, click on **TM1**, then select **Print Report**. From the **Print Report Wizard** dialog, you can select the desired options and click on **Next** to step through and set up all of the report options. Then click on **Finish**.
- You can use the report wizard to select any (or all) of the worksheets from the current Excel workbook to include in your report.
- TM1 Report Wizard will list the sheet name and title dimensions of your slice.
- TM1 Report Wizard can be used to control the number and grouping of worksheets in the report.
- The final step in using TM1 Report Wizard to create a report is to select a print destination of Printer, Excel file, or PDF file.
- The available printing options include the printer name, number of copies, print to file, and collate. TM1 Web allows access to cube data, the ability to view and edit via Excel reports, drill, pivot, select, and filter the TM1 data, cube data sourced charts, and even some TM1 Server Administrator tasks.
- TM1 Web consists of the **Navigation** pane on the left and the **Content** pane on the right. The **Navigation** pane contains a list of available TM1 applications, views, and a list of server object properties. TM1 Web's **Content** pane displays the cube views and websheets that you have access to.

- TM1 Web allows access and provides the ability to present TM1 data using Websheets, TM1 Web Cube Viewer, and TM1 Charts.
- By publishing an Excel worksheet from TM1 to an application folder, other users can view the worksheet by using a web browser.
- TM1 Web supports a variety of customizable chart types. To view cube data in TM1 Web in chart format, you can click on **View Chart**, **View Chart and Grid**, or **View Grid from the toolbar**.
- From the TM1 Web chart display, you can click on **Chart Properties** to change the chart type, colors, legend, and 3D view elements.

Self-Test

- **Question**: For the most part, what are the types of information in TM1?

  Response: The information will be trended over time, compared between different time periods, and forecasted for future time periods.

- **Question**: What are the most basic methods for browsing data in TM1 cubes?

  Response: The most basic methods for browsing data in TM1 cubes is by using either Cube Viewer or In-Spreadsheet Browser.

- **Question**: What programming is required to implement or otherwise set up for TM1 Cube Viewer?

  Response Cube Viewer does not require programming to be implemented. It works for all cubes in a TM1 instance to which the logged in user has access.

- **Question**: What are the steps to browse data in TM1 Cube Viewer?

  Response The following steps can be followed to browse data in Cube Viewer:

  a. Open TM1 Server Explorer.
  b. In the **Tree** pane, select the cube you want to browse.
  c. Click on the cube and select **Browse....** and then press *F9* or click on **Recalculate** to display the cell values.

- **Question**: Can Cube Viewer be changed or customized?

  Response: With mouse clicks, the cube view of the data can be easily customized to meet your requirements.

- **Question**: How is the ISB or In-Spreadsheet Browser implemented in TM1?

  Response: In-Spreadsheet Browser (ISB) does not require programming to be implemented. However, it may be up to you to configure what browsing method TM1 will use as the default browser—Cube Viewer or In-Spreadsheet Browser.

- **Question**: What information can be displayed from TM1 Cube Viewer? How can it be changed?

  Response: The information displayed in TM1 Cube Viewer is as follows:

  - Stack dimensions to see more detail along the columns or rows of a view
  - Drill down on the consolidated elements displayed in the view to see the underlying detail
  - Change the title dimension elements in the view to access a completely different view of cube data
  - Drill-through the view to the detailed data

- **Question**: How do you stack title dimensions as a row dimension in Cube Viewer?

  Response: Click on the element name in the title dimension and drag that element name to the right or left of a row dimension name.

- **Question**: How do you stack title dimensions as a column dimension in Cube Viewer?

  Response: Click on the element name in the title dimension and drag that element name to the right or left of a column dimension name.

- **Question**: How do you change title elements displayed in Cube Viewer?

  Response: Click an element name arrow, select an element, and press *F9*.

- **Question**: How do you access detailed level data for a selected cell of data in Cube Viewer?

  Response: A drill TI process and drill association rule must be implemented.

- **Question**: How do you save a view from TM1 Cube Viewer for later use?

  Response: To save a view from Cube Viewer, you click on **File** and then select **Save**. TM1 will prompt you with the **TM1 Save View** dialog.

- **Question**: How are cube views displayed to the user in TM1 Server Explorer?

  Response: TM1 Server Explorer displays view names beneath the cube with which they are associated. Icons will indicate whether a saved view is a public or private view.

- **Question**: What are the most common features for formatting data in a TM1 cube view?

  Response: The most common features provided by TM1 to format data displayed in a cube view are as follows:

  - Zero suppression
  - Cell formatting
  - Column orientations

- **Question**: How do you turn on zero suppression in a TM1 cube view?

  Response: For row suppression, you can click on **Options | Suppress Zeroes On Rows**. For column suppression, you can click on **Options | Suppress Zeroes On Columns**.

- **Question**: What is a common method to customize the display of data in a cube view?

  Response: To customize the display of data within a cube view cell, the Format attribute can be used.

- **Question**: How are column elements displayed in the TM1 cube views?

  Response: Column elements are displayed left to right by default in TM1. You may change to right to left by clicking the menu option **Layout Right to Left** (or **Layout Left to Right**, depending upon the current view).

- **Question**: How do you create a TM1 slice?

  Response: To slice a view from Cube Viewer to an Excel worksheet, you can click on **File** and then select **Slice**.

- **Question**: How do you create a TM1 snapshot?

  Response: To create a snapshot from Cube Viewer, you can click on **File** and then select **Snapshot**.

- **Question**: What is a key point of TM1 Active Forms?

  Response: Active Form reports retain the ability to expand and collapse row dimension consolidations in TM1 views while allowing you to use native Excel features and functions to create complex reports.

- **Question**: Can Active Forms be used in TM1 Web?

  Response: TM1 Active Forms are supported in TM1 Web, if an Active Form is added to TM1 Applications, that form can be accessed and used in TM1 Web.

- **Question**: What TM1 functions are utilized to create Active Forms?

  Response: There are a special group of TM1 worksheet functions that are used for the support of Active Forms:

  - `TM1RptView`
  - `TM1RptTitle`
  - `TM1RptRow`
  - `TM1RptFilter`
  - `TM1RptElLev`
  - `TM1RptElIsExpanded`
  - `TM1RptElIsConsolidated`

- **Question**: How does one create an Active Form report?

  Response: The most basic method of creating an Active Form report is by using Cube Viewer. From the menu, you can click on **File** and then select **Active Form**.

- **Question**: How do you refresh an Active Form?

  Response: You can refresh the data displayed in it by pressing *F9*.

- **Question**: Is it possible to remove an Active Form from a worksheet?

  Response: To remove an Active Form from a worksheet, you must click in the data area of an Active Form and then click on **Active Form** | **Delete**.

- **Question**: What formatting features are available in TM1 Active Forms?

  Response: Active Forms currently support the features such as suppression of zeros, data spread and hold, drilling, edit of row subsets, save to static list, title element change, dependent sections, and insertion of columns.

- **Question**: Where is formatting defined in a TM1 Active Form?

  Response: Active Form formatting is defined directly in the worksheet containing the form.

- **Question**: Describe the format area of a TM1 Active Form.

  Response: Active Form formatting is defined via the format range which is hidden within the Active Form worksheet. This hidden range is revealed by clicking on the Active Form and then selecting the **Show Format Area** option.

- **Question**: How is the formatting range in a TM1 Active Form changed?

  Response: To change the formatting from what TM1 provides as a default format, you can apply all standard cell formats available in the **Excel Format Cells** dialog box.

- **Question**: When are changes to the Active Forms formatting visible?

  Response: All changes made in the format range will be applied to all cells in the Active Forms worksheet that use the corresponding format definition which is updated when you recalculate the form.

- **Question**: What is required to apply formatting that you implemented as an additional Active Form formatting?

  Response: If you defined an additional format, column A of the first row in your Active Form must contain a function that resolves to one of the format definition labels in the format range.

- **Question**: What may be considered as the three main limitations of Active Forms?

  Response: The three main limitations of Active Forms are as follows:

  - Worksheet names cannot include a dash (-) character
  - Merging cells in an Active Form always requires a rebuild of the worksheet or workbook
  - Active Forms require at least one row dimension

- **Question**: What are some options for TM1 Print Report Wizard output formats?

  Response: TM1 Print Report Wizard can be used to print reports or save reports as Excel or PDF documents.

- **Question**: How do you access TM1 Print Report Wizard?

  Response: To use TM1 Print Report wizard you have to perform the following steps:

  a. From the menu bar, click on **TM1**, and then select **Print Report**.
  b. From the **Print Report Wizard** dialog, you can select the desired options and click on **Next** to step through and set up all of the report options.
  c. Then, click on **Finish**.

- **Question**: Can the TM1 Print Report Wizard support multiple worksheets within a workbook?

  Response: You can use the TM1 Print Report Wizard to select any (or all) of the worksheets from the current Excel workbook to include in your report. In the wizard, you have to select the checkbox of the worksheet that you want to include in the report or you can click on **Select All** to include all of the worksheets in the current workbook in the report.

- **Question**: Describe the abilities of TM1 Web.

  Response: TM1 Web allows access to cube data, provides the ability to view and edit via Excel reports, drill, pivot, select, and filter the TM1 data, cube data sourced charts, and even some TM1 Server Administrator tasks all through a client's web browser.

- **Question**: Describe the TM1 Web view.

  Response: TM1 Web consists of the **Navigation** pane on the left and the **Content** pane on the right. The **Navigation** pane contains a list of available TM1 applications, views, and a list of server object properties. TM1 Web's **Content** pane displays the cube views and websheets for which you have access.

- **Question**: What is the process to share worksheets within TM1 Web?

  Response: By publishing an Excel worksheet from TM1 to an application folder, other users can view the worksheet by using a web browser.

- **Question**: How does one access TM1 Web Cube Viewer?

  Response: To utilize Cube Viewer within TM1 Web, you can log in to TM1 Web and open **Views** in the **Navigation** pane, then expand the cube views that you are interested in and click on the view that you wish to access.

Index

Symbols

A

B

C

D

E

F

G

H

I

K

L

M

N

O

P

Q

R

S

T

V

W

Y

Thank you for buying
IBM Cognos TM1 Developer's Certification Guide

About Packt Publishing

Packt, pronounced 'packed', published its first book "Mastering phpMyAdmin for Effective MySQL Management" in April 2004 and subsequently continued to specialize in publishing highly focused books on specific technologies and solutions.

Our books and publications share the experiences of your fellow IT professionals in adapting and customizing today's systems, applications, and frameworks. Our solution based books give you the knowledge and power to customize the software and technologies you're using to get the job done. Packt books are more specific and less general than the IT books you have seen in the past. Our unique business model allows us to bring you more focused information, giving you more of what you need to know, and less of what you don't.

Packt is a modern, yet unique publishing company, which focuses on producing quality, cutting-edge books for communities of developers, administrators, and newbies alike. For more information, please visit our website: `www.packtpub.com`.

About Packt Enterprise

In 2010, Packt launched two new brands, Packt Enterprise and Packt Open Source, in order to continue its focus on specialization. This book is part of the Packt Enterprise brand, home to books published on enterprise software - software created by major vendors, including (but not limited to) IBM, Microsoft and Oracle, often for use in other corporations. Its titles will offer information relevant to a range of users of this software, including administrators, developers, architects, and end users.

Writing for Packt

We welcome all inquiries from people who are interested in authoring. Book proposals should be sent to author@packtpub.com. If your book idea is still at an early stage and you would like to discuss it first before writing a formal book proposal, contact us; one of our commissioning editors will get in touch with you.

We're not just looking for published authors; if you have strong technical skills but no writing experience, our experienced editors can help you develop a writing career, or simply get some additional reward for your expertise.

[PACKT] enterprise
professional expertise distilled
PUBLISHING

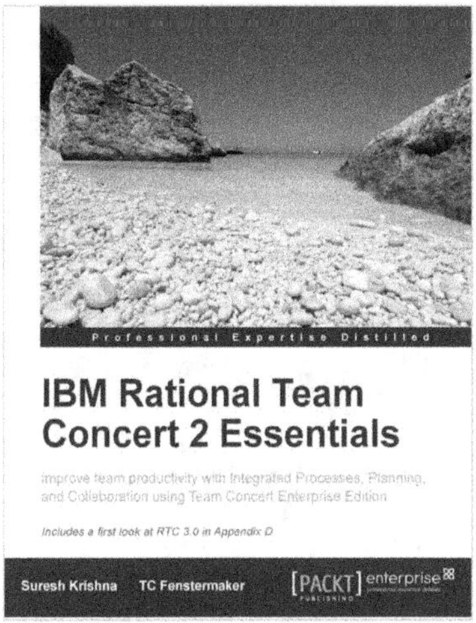

IBM Rational Team Concert 2 Essentials

ISBN: 978-1-84968-160-5 Paperback: 308 pages

Improve team productivity with Integrated Processes, Planning, and Collaboration using Team Concert Enterprise Edition

1. Understand the core features and techniques of Rational Team Concert and Jazz platform through a real-world Book Manager Application
2. Expand your knowledge of software development challenges and find out how Rational Team Concert solves your tech, team, and collaboration worries
3. Complete overview and understanding of the Jazz Platform, Rational Team Concert, and other products built on the Jazz Platform

---

IBM Cognos TM1 Cookbook

ISBN: 978-1-84968-210-7 Paperback: 490 pages

Build real world planning, budgeting, and forecasting solutions with a collection of over 60 simple but incredibly efective recipes

1. A comprehensive developer's guide for planning, building, and managing practical applications with IBM TM1
2. No prior knowledge of TM1 expected
3. Complete coverage of all the important aspects of IBM TM1 in carefully planned step-by-step practical demos

Please check **www.PacktPub.com** for information on our titles

www.ingramcontent.com/pod-product-compliance
Lightning Source LLC
LaVergne TN
LVHW080043210926
848481LV00011B/3266
9781849684903